BOOK 2

THE
CIRCLE
TRILOGY

RED is the second book in the Circle Trilogy.

It began in **BLACK** with a man named Thomas Hunter and the birth of evil in a world he never knew existed. Now he alone stands between the annihilation of two worlds separated only by his dreams.

In one, a terrorist has released the Raison Strain, a mutated virus that will infect millions within days and kill billions within weeks. There is no vaccine. There is no antidote. Thomas leads the search for the one person who may be able to create one if time, and his ability to stay alive, doesn't run out first.

In the other world fifteen years have passed since Tanis, the firstborn of men, entered the Black Forest, betraying his people and unleashing the Shataiki on the land. The Colored Forest is now a wasteland, replaced by searing desert, and the people have been scattered.

Some found their way to the few forests that survived, but most ventured deep into the desert where they were overcome with a disease that poisoned their minds and bodies. They would come to be known as the Horde, nomadic warriors bent on one goal—waging war on what remains of the Forest People.

Thomas, now a respected general, leads the remnant of the Forest Guard in this war. A war they must not lose, but may not be able to win. Outnumbered, but not outmatched, they ride into the desert to meet their enemies and fight to save what remains of their way of life.

THE HORDE'S ATTACK CAME FROM THE CANYON LANDS.
BY ITSELF, NOT SO UNUSUAL. THIRTEEN YEARS OF WAR HAD SOAKED THE SAND HERE WITH THE BLOOD OF BATTLE.
BUT, NEVER HAS THE HORDE GOTTEN SO CLOSE TO THE FORESTS.
UNTIL NOW.
THEY HAVE GROWN STRONGER. BOLDER.
MIKIL?
A HUNDRED THOUSAND. MAYBE MORE.

HOW DID THEY GET SO CLOSE WITHOUT US KNOWING?
THE MAIN BODY IS MOVING SOUTH, ALONG THE CLIFFS.
THEY'RE TRYING TO ENGAGE US IN THE NATALGA GAP. THE MAIN FORCE WILL FLANK US.
AND THEY LOOK TO SUCCEED.
ONLY IF WE LET THEM, WILLIAM.
THEY HAVE NUMBERS ON THEIR SIDE, BUT ELYON IS ON OURS. AND THAT IS ENOUGH.
THEY ARE A CURSED PEOPLE, DISEASED AND ROTTING.
SCABS.

WILLIAM, TAKE THE CANYON TO THE FOREST. BRING THE REINFORCEMENTS UP.
FORGIVE ME FOR POINTING OUT THE OBVIOUS, BUT TAKING THEM HERE WILL END... BADLY.
THE HIGH GROUND OF THE GAP FAVORS US. WE'LL ENGAGE THEM THERE.
BEFORE MORE MEN ARRIVE? IT'S SUICIDE.
WE CAN HOLD THEM. YOU JUST BRING THE OTHERS.
ONCE THE MEN ARE ON THE MOVE HAVE CIPHUS EVACUATE THE TRIBE TO THE NORTHERN VILLAGES.
I'M A WARRIOR SIR, NOT A MESSENGER.
I'M NOT ASKING, I'M TELLING.
I NEED YOU TO DO THIS. YOU'RE THE FASTEST RIDER. GO *NOW*.
HIYAAA!
WELL, MY FRIENDS, YOU SIGNED ON FOR A FIGHT.
MAY ELYON'S STRENGTH KEEP US.
ELYON'S STRENGTH!

SIR! I BRING WORD FROM THE SOUTHERN FOREST!
GO ON, QUICKLY.
THE HORDE HAS BREACHED THE FOREST.
HOW LONG AGO?
THREE HOURS AGO. IT'S SAID THEY'RE LED BY MARTYN.
GENERAL OF QURONG'S ARMIES.
SOME SAY HE PRACTICES THE BLACK ARTS, THAT HE IS GUIDED BY TEELEH HIMSELF.
HOW MANY GUARD?
FEWER THAN A THOUSAND, AND THEY ARE IN RETREAT.
WHO'S IN CHARGE?
JAMOUS.
JAMOUS? *JAMOUS* IS IN RETREAT?
IF A WARRIOR LIKE JAMOUS IS RETREATING, THE THREAT MUST BE REAL.
THERE WAS ALSO A WARRIOR NAMED JUSTIN THERE.
SIR?
JUSTIN. SINCE THE DAY HE DEFIED THOMAS AND DESERTED THE GUARD, HE HAS BEEN KNOWN AS THE TRAITOR.
SOME SAY HE PLANS TO TAKE OVER THE FOREST COUNCIL.
HAS HE BETRAYED US AND BROUGHT THE ENEMY TO OUR DOOR?

I WILL BEG ELYON FOR YOUR SAFETY TODAY. I WILL BEG ELYON FOR THE SAFETY OF US ALL.
IF ANY SHOULD DIE, LET IT BE THAT TRAITOR, JUSTIN.
RIDER! WORD TO WILLIAM AND CIPHUS!
SEND A THOUSAND MEN TO THE SOUTHERN FOREST. IF WE ARE OVERTAKEN HERE, WE WILL MEET IN THE THIRD FOREST TO THE NORTH.
GO!
HOLD... HOLD.
ELYON'S STRENGTH...
NOW!

AAAAH!
UURGHH
SLORCH!
SLURPP!
MIKIL! ON YOUR RIGHT!
THOMAS, THERE ARE TOO MANY...

EVEN IF WE HOLD THEM 'TIL NIGHTFALL, THEY'LL MARCH OVER US TOMORROW.
WHAT'S THE PLAN?
I DON'T HAVE ONE.
IF YOU DON'T COME UP WITH ONE SOON, YOU MAY NEVER PLAN AGAIN!
WE CAN'T JUST STAND HERE.
I'M NOT JUST STANDING HERE! I'M THINKING!
WHO DO YOU THINK I AM? ELYON?
DO YOU THINK I CAN JUST CLAP MY HANDS AND BRING THE CLIFF DOWN ON THEM?
THAT'S IT!
WHAT? WHAT IS IT?
I HAVEN'T EATEN THE RHAMBUTAN FRUIT TODAY. IT'S ALL THAT KEEPS ME FROM DREAMING. KNOCK ME OUT.
WHAT? ARE YOU CRAZY? YOU WANT TO NAP IN THE MIDDLE OF A BATTLE!
NO. THERE IS A WAY--IN THE BOOK OF HISTORIES--TO BRING THE CLIFF DOWN.
BUT I NEED TO DREAM AND REMEMBER. IT'S AN ORDER--HIT ME!
HOW LONG DO I LET YOU SLEEP?
WAKE ME IN TEN MINUTES.
THIS IS INSANE...
NOW, MIKIL!

BANGKOK
HUNTER HAD BLED IN HIS SLEEP? WAS BLEEDING IN HIS SLEEP.
IS HE DEAD?
NO. HE'S BREATHING.
BUT, I DON'T REMEMBER THESE SCARS.
NO MATTER.
IT ENDS NOW.
GOOD BYE, MR. HUNTER.

BAM!
THOMAS!
1020
1010
1005
THOMAS!
1020
KARA, MEET CARLOS.

HE HASN'T HEARD ABOUT THE ANTI-VIRUS WE HAVE. SO HE THINKS IT'S SAFE TO KILL ME. I THOUGHT IT WOULD SOUND MORE CONVINCING COMING FROM YOU.
ANTI---? THOMAS YOU'RE BLEEDING...
I ONLY HAVE TO BUY HER A COUPLE SECONDS.
KARA, LISTEN TO ME.
UNDER THE BED.
YOU WON'T HAVE MUCH TIME.
GO!
SCHLITT
THWACK!

BLAM!
KRESSHHH!
BLAM!
WHRACK!

THOMAS!
THOMAS...
WAKE UP THOMAS.
WAKE UP!
UNHHH
THOMAS, WAKE UP...
DID YOU GET IT?
GET WHAT?
I KNEW IT! I KNEW YOU WOULDN'T GET IT!
WAIT! HOW LONG HAVE I BEEN UNCONSCIOUS FOR?
FIVE MINUTES!
FIVE? I SAID TEN!
WHY DID YOU WAKE ME?
I DIDN'T! YOU WOKE ON YOUR OWN.

MAYBE ELYON WOKE YOU TO GO LEAD YOUR MEN.
NO! I HAVE TO GO BACK!
GO BACK WHERE?
I DIDN'T HAVE TIME.
I HAVE TO GET BACK TO LEARN HOW TO MAKE EXPLOSIVES.
EX-- THIS IS NONSENSE! WHAT WOULD YOU HAVE ME DO?
HIT YOU ON THE HEAD WITH ANOTHER ROCK?
YES!
IT WORKED! I'M DREAMING AGAIN!
I WAS THERE, MIKIL!
I FOUGHT A MAN WHO WAS TRYING TO SHOOT ME WITH A GUN.
A GUN, IT'S A TYPE OF EXPLOSIVE DEVICE.
THIS MAN, CARLOS, HE FIGHTS--HE'S VERY GOOD.
I THINK HE KNOCKED ME OUT. THAT'S WHY I AWOKE HERE.

THOMAS, YOU MUST REJOIN THE BATTLE!
WE NEED A DECISION. WE CAN'T HOLD THEM OFF MUCH LONGER.
...AND KARA WAS THERE.
MY SISTER... KARA.
MIKIL? DID I HAVE THIS CUT?
YOU MUST HAVE. I DON'T REMEMBER.
NO! IT WASN'T HERE WHEN I CAME UP.
NO ONE CUT ME WHILE I WAS SLEEPING?
OF COURSE NOT. THOMAS, WE DON'T HAVE TIME...

THEN IT'S FROM MY DREAMS!
WHAT? HOW IS THAT POSSIBLE?
THE CUT– IT'S FROM MY DREAMS!
YOU ARE MAKING NO SENSE, THOMAS!
HURRY! HIT ME!
NOW, MIKIL! I NEED TO GET BACK TO SAVE MY SISTER!
WHAT?
BUT... YOU DON'T HAVE A SISTER.
YES I DO! NOW HIT ME! ***JUST HIT ME!***
IT'S NOT WITHIN ME TO STRIKE MY COMMANDER TWICE IN THE SPACE OF TEN MINUTES, EVEN IF--
MIKIL YOU MUST, THERE IS NO OTHER WAY.
PRETEND I'M NOT YOUR COMMANDER. PRETEND I'M A SCAB AND SMELL OF ROTTEN MEAT AND I WILL---

THOMAS, WAKE UP. ARE YOU OK? GAINS JUST CALLED. I TOLD HIM ABOUT CARLOS - HE WANTS TO SEE US.
YEAH, I'M OK. LET'S GO, HE NEEDS MY HELP, AND I NEED HIS.
IF GAINS IS LOOKING FOR US, THEY MUST HAVE MORE NEWS OF THE VIRUS.
LET'S HOPE SO.
MR. GAINES WILL BE WITH YOU SHORTLY.
CARLOS WILL BE BACK...
GAINES WAS RIGHT ABOUT GETTING MORE SECURITY FOR MY SUITE.
BUT WHAT I DON'T UNDERSTAND IS... THIRTEEN YEARS?
SOMETHING LIKE THAT.
YOU'VE BEEN IN THE OTHER WORLD FOR THAT LONG? YOU'RE SURE?
QUITE SURE.
HOW IS THAT POSSIBLE? YOU'RE NOT THIRTEEN YEARS OLDER, ARE YOU?
MY BODY ISN'T, NAY-
NAY?
SORRY.
NAY... SOUNDS OLD.

I'M ALMOST FORTY THERE.
AND HONESTLY, I FEEL FORTY HERE AS WELL.
SO THESE WOUNDS ARE A DEFINITE CHANGE IN THE RULES BETWEEN THE TWO REALITIES.
KNOWLEDGE AND SKILL ALWAYS TRANSFERRED BOTH WAYS, BUT BEFORE THE COLORED FOREST TURNED BLACK, YOUR INJURIES IN THAT WORLD DIDN'T CROSS OVER HERE, JUST HERE TO THERE.
NOW, EVIDENTLY, IT GOES BOTH WAYS.
BUT, IT MAKES SENSE. BLOOD HAS TO DO WITH LIFE.
THAT'S THE CONNECTION.
BUT WHEN YOU FIRST HIT YOUR HEAD–WHEN THIS FIRST THING STARTED–IT BLED IN BOTH WORLDS.
MAYBE I REALLY DID WOUND IN BOTH WORLDS AT THE SAME TIME. MAYBE THAT'S WHAT OPENED THIS GATEWAY.
I KNOW IT SOUNDS CRAZY.
YOU'RE THE ONLY GATEWAY. WE'RE TALKING ABOUT YOUR KNOWLEDGE, YOUR SKILLS. YOUR BLOOD.
CORRECT.

IT WOULD EXPLAIN WHY YOU'VE AGED THERE BUT NOT HERE. YOU GET CUT THERE AND YOU GET CUT HERE, BUT DON'T AGE THE SAME, OR GAIN WEIGHT OR SWEAT THE SAME.
ONLY SPECIFIC EVENTS TIED TO THE SPILLING OF BLOOD SHOW UP IN BOTH REALITIES.
AND YOU'RE A GENERAL?
GENERAL OF THE FOREST GUARD, THOMAS OF HUNTER.
HOW DID THAT HAPPEN?
IT'S A LONG STORY THAT GOES BACK TO WHEN WE FLED THE COLORED FOREST.
AFTER THE SHATAIKI SPREAD THEIR POISON THROUGH THE FOREST A TERRIBLE DISEASE OVER TOOK THE POPULATION.
IT MAKES THE SKIN FLAKE AND CRACK, AND STINK LIKE ROTTEN EGGS.
BUT ELYON MADE A WAY FOR US TO LIVE WITHOUT THE EFFECTS OF THIS DISEASE. SEVEN FORESTS–REGULAR ONES, NOT COLORED–STILL STAND AND EACH HAS A LAKE.
WE MUST BATHE REGULARLY AND KEEP THE LAKES FROM BEING DEFILED WITH BLOOD.
AND THE PROPHECY?
THAT ELYON WILL BRING DOWN THE HORDE WITH ONE BLOW? MAYBE DYNAMITE IS ELYON'S ANSWER. THAT'S WHY I'M HERE. I GOT MIKIL TO KNOCK ME OUT.
SO I TAKE IT YOU'RE STILL DREAMING?

MR. GAINS.
GOOD. WE'RE GOING TO NEED THESE DREAMS OF YOURS.
NEVER IMAGINED I WOULD EVER SAY SOME-THING LIKE THAT, BUT THEN AGAIN, I NEVER IMAGINED WE WOULD FACE SUCH A MONSTROUS EVIL.
CAN I GET EITHER OF YOU A DRINK?
NO THANKS.
I HATE TO ADMIT IT BUT WE'VE UNDERESTIMATED YOU FROM THE BEGINNING, THOMAS.
I CAN ASSURE YOU— THAT HAS JUST CHANGED.
I'LL CUT TO THE CHASE. LAST NIGHT AT BANGKOK INTERNATIONAL A MAN WAS REPORTED HARASSING SEVERAL FLIGHT ATTENDANTS, BEING UNUSUALLY FRIENDLY-SHAKING HANDS AND HUGGING STRANGERS AND SO ON—ALL OVER THE AIRPORT.
WE FOUND HIS BELONG-INGS AND A BRIEFCASE IN ONE OF THE AIRPORT TOILETS. LAST NIGHT WE CONCLUDED AN ANALYSIS OF THAT BRIEFCASE.
ANY GUESS AS TO WHAT THEY FOUND?
THE RAISON STRAIN.

AS PROMISED BY VALBORG SVENSSON, AND AS PREDICTED BY YOU. YOU ARE A VERY IMPORTANT MAN, THOMAS, WHICH IS WHY WE NEED TO HEAD TO WASHINGTON.
D.C.? WHY?
THE PRESIDENT WANTS YOU TO MEET WITH THE TASK FORCE HE'S ASSEMBLING NOW.
I'M NOT SURE YOU UNDERSTAND THE FULL EXTENT OF WHAT'S GOING ON HERE. THE VIRUS IS AIRBORNE.
BY THE TIME WE GET TO WASHINGTON, HALF OF THAILAND WILL BE INFECTED. IF WE ARE NOT ALREADY INFECTED, WE WILL BE SOON. TIME IS RUNNING OUT.
ANY WORD ON MONIQUE?
NO.
SVENSSON MAY NOT HAVE THE ANTIVIRUS YET, BUT WITH HER HELP, HE WILL.
WHEN THAT HAPPENS, WE'RE FINISHED. WE NEED TO FIND HER.
MONIQUE IS NOT A PRIORITY. AT THIS POINT IT'S OUT OF MY HANDS–
SEE? THE SAME PROBLEM AS BEFORE. I TELL YOU SOMETHING AND YOU DON'T LISTEN.
WHY WILL ANYONE IN WASHINGTON BE ANY DIFFERENT?
I *AM* LISTENING TO YOU.
I'M SAYING THAT THE PRESIDENT HAS TAKEN THIS OVER. I'M NOT THE ONE WHO NEEDS CONVINCING.
FINE. I'LL GO, FOR MONIQUE'S SAKE. ON ONE CONDITION.

I'M NOT SURE YOU REALIZE THE FULL EXTENT OF WHAT I'M FACING IN THE OTHER WORLD, MERTON. I NEED HELP.
THEN LET ME HELP YOU.
I'M LEADING WHAT REMAINS OF MY ARMY, THE FOREST GUARD, AGAINST AN INCREDIBLY UNEQUAL BATTLE WITH THE HORDE.
IF I DON'T FIND A WAY TO BRING DOWN A CLIFF ON TOP OF THEM, OUR ARMY, AND THE WOMEN AND CHILDREN IN THE NEARBY FOREST, WILL ALL BE SLAUGHTERED.
THAT MAY SEEM LIKE A LOT OF HOGWASH TO YOU, BUT IF I DIE THERE, I DIE HERE.
I'LL DO EVERYTHING I CAN TO HELP YOU, IF YOU'LL HELP ME STAY ALIVE.
I WILL, THOMAS. FOR THE SAKE OF YOUR CREDIBILITY, I SUGGEST THAT WE DON'T SHARE ALL THESE DETAILS WITH THE FOLKS IN WASHINGTON.
UNDERSTOOD.
WE'RE IN A CANYON LAND. ROCK RICH IN COPPER, TIN ORES. I NEED TO FIND A WAY TO MAKE AN EXPLOSIVE.
BLACK POWDER.
NOT DYNAMITE?
BLACK POWDER WAS FIRST MADE BY COMBINING COMMON ELEMENTS.
I'LL GET THE C.I.A. TO SEND YOU A HOW-TO AND YOU CAN REVIEW ON THE WAY TO D.C.
LATER
GAINS WAS RIGHT. TAKE A LOOK AT THE THREE INGREDIENTS. THERE ARE SOME SUBSTITUTES TOO; YOU COULD USE THE SUGAR FOR THE CHARCOAL.
I HAVE TO MEMORIZE THIS, AND THE RATIOS.
LET'S JUST HOPE I CAN FIND WHAT I NEED.
ELYON'S STRENGTH.
ELYON'S STRENGTH.

WAKE UP.
WAKE UP!
OW! HEY! I AM AWAKE.
THERE ISN'T MUCH TIME. WE'RE BEING CUT TO PIECES. I HOPE YOU FOUND WHAT YOU'RE LOOKING FOR.
I DID. BUT, WE'RE GOING TO NEED SOME HELP.
I HOPE THIS IDEA OF YOURS WORKS, WHATEVER IT IS.
IT WILL.
LET'S MOVE. WE'VE GOT TO ROUND UP SOME OF THE MEN.
IF THERE ARE ANY LEFT TO ROUND UP.

MIKIL, YOUR SKIN.
I KNOW. NONE OF US HAVE BATHED IN DAYS. OUR SKIN IS BEGINNING TO TURN.
THE DISEASE...
...IT SPREADS QUICKLY. I WAS STRANDED ONCE FOR FOUR DAYS. MY WATER WAS GONE BY THE SECOND DAY. BY THE THIRD DAY, I WAS LIKE THEM.
BY THE TIME SOME SCABS FOUND ME, I'D CHANGED.
WHO ARE YOU, AND WHAT BUSINESS DO YOU HAVE HERE?
MY NAME IS ROLAND. I'M ON A PERSONAL MISSION FOR QURONG.
IS THAT SO, AND WHAT IS THIS MISSION OF YOURS?
I DIDN'T CRAVE FRESH WATER ANY MORE. THE SAND DIDN'T HURT. THE GRAY SKIN... WASN'T SO BAD.
I CANNOT SAY.
AH, OF COURSE NOT.
ARE YOU MARRIED?
NO, MY LADY.
I AM CHELISE, DAUGHTER OF QURONG. COME, I WOULD LIKE TO LEARN MORE ABOUT YOU.
LET ME COMPLETE MY MISSION. LEND ME A HORSE AND I WILL RETURN TO YOU TOMORROW.
I MADE IT BACK TO THE LAKES BY THE END OF THE FOURTH DAY.
THE PAIN FROM ELYON'S WATER ON THE DISEASE WAS ALMOST UNBEARABLE.
THE DISEASE WASHED AWAY, BUT THE MEMORY OF CHELISE REMAINED.
THE DAUGHTER OF THE MIGHTY QURONG.
IN A STRANGE WAY SHE WAS BEAUTIFUL.
AND THE ONLY THING THAT SEPARATED HER, FROM MIKIL OR ANY OTHER WOMAN, WAS ELYON'S WATER.

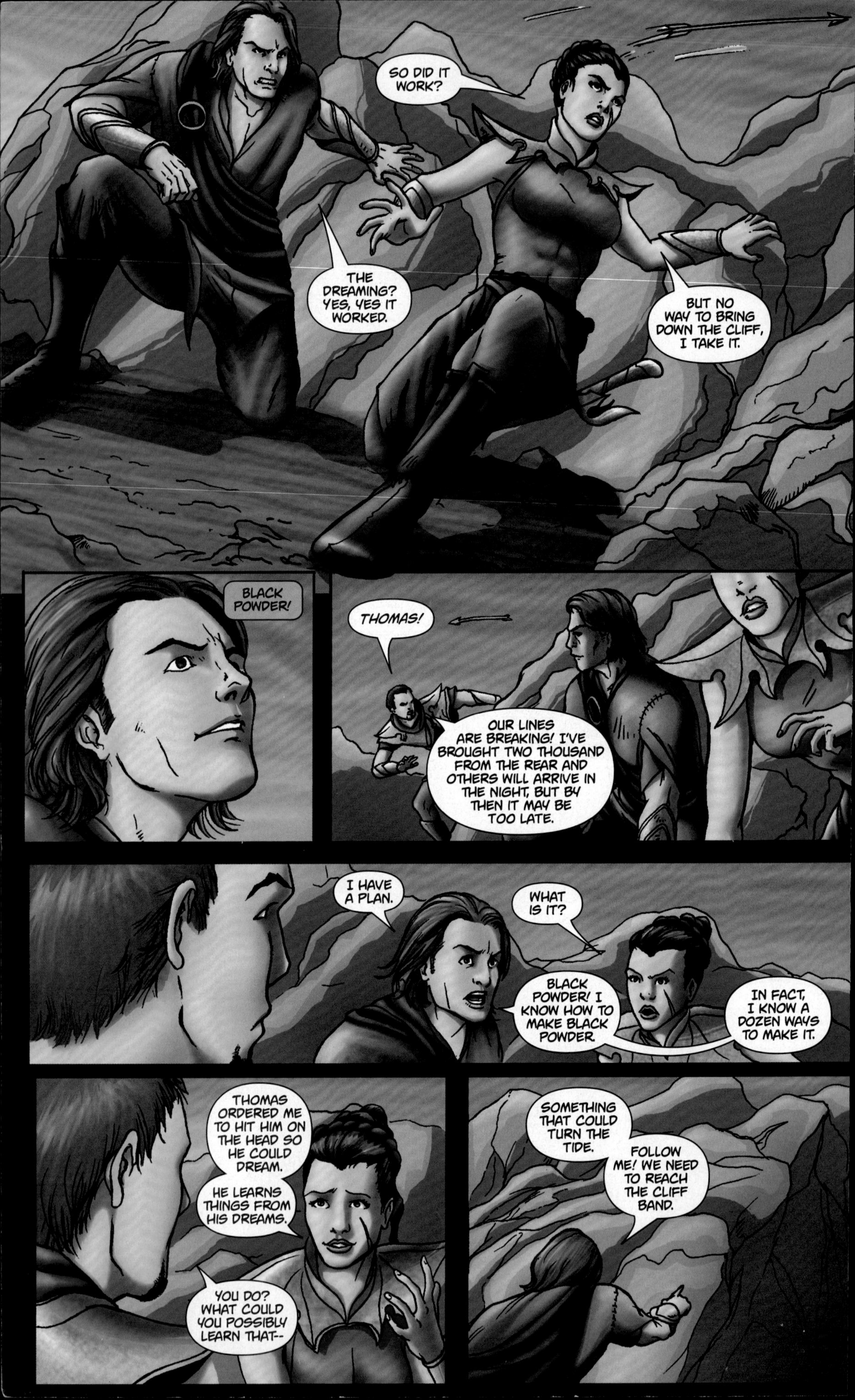
SO DID IT WORK?
THE DREAMING? YES, YES IT WORKED.
BUT NO WAY TO BRING DOWN THE CLIFF, I TAKE IT.
BLACK POWDER!
THOMAS!
OUR LINES ARE BREAKING! I'VE BROUGHT TWO THOUSAND FROM THE REAR AND OTHERS WILL ARRIVE IN THE NIGHT, BUT BY THEN IT MAY BE TOO LATE.
I HAVE A PLAN.
WHAT IS IT?
BLACK POWDER! I KNOW HOW TO MAKE BLACK POWDER.
IN FACT, I KNOW A DOZEN WAYS TO MAKE IT.
THOMAS ORDERED ME TO HIT HIM ON THE HEAD SO HE COULD DREAM.
HE LEARNS THINGS FROM HIS DREAMS.
YOU DO? WHAT COULD YOU POSSIBLY LEARN THAT--
SOMETHING THAT COULD TURN THE TIDE.
FOLLOW ME! WE NEED TO REACH THE CLIFF BAND.

LET ME GET THIS STRAIGHT. YOU PLAN TO DEFEAT THE HORDE BY SPRINKLING POWDER ON THEM?
HAVE YOU GONE MAD?
HE PLANS TO BRING THE CLIFF DOWN ON THEIR HEADS! RIGHT THOMAS?
ESSENTIALLY, YES. BLACK POWDER IS AN EXPLOSIVE, A FIRE THAT BURNS VERY FAST.
IF WE PACK IT INTO THE CRACK AT THE TOP OF THE CLIFF AND IGNITE IT, THE ENTIRE ROCKFACE MIGHT COLLAPSE.
YOU ACTUALLY... KNOW HOW TO MAKE THIS BLACK POWDER FROM YOUR DREAMS?
YES.
WHAT DO WE DO?
IT'S COMPOSED OF THREE BASIC INGREDIENTS: CHARCOAL, SULFUR AND SALTPETER.
WE HAVE TO FIND THESE THREE INGREDIENTS, PREPARE THEM IN TIGHTLY PACKED POUCHES, LOWER THEM---
WHAT IS SULFUR?
SALTPETER?

THIS IS THE MOST ABSURD THING I'VE EVER HEARD!
WE'RE ALMOST OUT OF TIME. IF WE LOSE HERE THE ENTIRE FOREST WILL FALL. ALL I'M ASKING FOR IS YOUR TRUST AND A LITTLE HOPE.
CHARCOAL WE HAVE, RIGHT? WE BURN IT. A FEW FAST RIDERS CAN RETRIEVE AN AMPLE SUPPLY AND HAVE IT HERE BY MIDNIGHT.
SULFUR IS FOUND IN CAVES LIKE THE ONES AT THE NORTH END OF THE GAP. SEND SOME MEN.
WE'LL NEED TO BREAK OFF THE CONES, HEAT THEM IN A LARGE FIRE AND PRAY THAT SULFUR FLOWS FROM THE PORES.
WHAT ABOUT THE SALT?
SALTPETER. IT'S A WHITE, TRANSLUCENT MINERAL.
AND WHERE DO WE FIND THIS?
IN THE CAVES.
SIR! WILLIAM THINKS HE MAY HAVE FOUND THE MINERAL YOU SEEK!
NOW WHAT?
NOW WE GRIND THEM TO A FINE POWDER, CAREFULLY MIX THEM, PACK THEM INTO SMALL SACKS, AND PRAY TO ELYON THAT THERE'S ENOUGH FORCE TO DO SOME DAMAGE.
WILL IT WORK?
WE WILL KNOW SOON ENOUGH.

SEVEN THOUSAND JOINED THE BATTLE IN THE CANYON.
THREE THOUSAND FELL.
THIS IS OUR WORST DEFEAT EVER.
AND IF THIS LITTLE TRICK DOESN'T WORK, THE WORST IS YET TO COME.
THE MEN HAVE PACKED THE POUCHES IN THE CRACKS ALONG THIS LEDGE JUST AS YOU ASKED.
GOOD. NOW LET'S HOPE THIS WORKS.
FIRE FROM DIRT. I WILL ADMIT, IT'S PRETTY IMPRESSIVE.
I HOPE SO.
HOW MANY ARE THERE ON EACH OF THE TWO CLIFFS?
TWENTY BOMBS, ON EACH CLIFF.
BOMBS?
THAT'S WHAT THEY ARE CALLED.
ARE WE READY?
YES. WHERE ARE YOU GOING?
TO POKE THE HORNET'S NEST.
TO THE HORDE? ALONE?
YES.
DESERT DWELLERS! MY NAME IS THOMAS OF HUNTER! IF YOU WISH TO LIVE, YOU WILL BRING ME YOUR LEADER!
IF HE IS A COWARD, THEN YOU WILL ALL DIE WHEN WE RAIN FIRE FROM THE SKIES AND BURN YOU TO CINDERS!

ARE YOU BLIND? LOOK AROUND YOU. YOUR DEAD LAY IN PILES.
MAGIC TRICKS WILL NOT SPARE YOUR MEN.
YOU DON'T KNOW THE FIRE ELYON HAS GIVEN US! RETREAT OR FACE HIS WRATH.
WE DO NOT FEAR YOUR PRECIOUS ELYON.
BRAC KROOM
NOW.
CHOOM

ELYON!
ELYON!
ELYON!
HUNTER!
HUNTER!
HUNTER!
SO TIRED. WE NEED TO BATHE, AND REST.
I NEED TO DREAM.

LANGLEY, VA.
PHIL GRANT, CIA DIRECTOR.
SIX MORE CITIES ARE INFECTED.
INCLUDING ST. PETERSBURG AS OF THIS MORNING.
WHAT ABOUT CLOSING THE AIRPORTS?
CDC RAN ANOTHER MODEL USING THE LATEST DATA. THEY SAY IT WON'T HELP AT THIS POINT.
THE ONLY THING THAT DOES MAKE SENSE NOW IS UNLOCKING YOUR MIND TO LEARN MORE FROM THIS OTHER WORLD.
YOU'RE SURE YOU HAVE NO INFORMATION, NONE AT ALL, ON WHERE SVENNSON MIGHT BE HOLED UP?
NONE. OR WHERE MONIQUE IS.
WITH ANY LUCK, DR. BANCROFT CAN STIMULATE THAT MEMORY OF YOURS AND WE CAN GET SOME ANSWERS.
LATER.
...SINCE THE BRAIN RECORDS EVERYTHING, IF WE HOOK YOU UP TO THESE WIRES HERE AND RECORD THE WAVE SIGNATURES, WE MAY BE ABLE TO GET SOMEWHERE.
PROBLEM IS, WE'RE A BIT FUZZY ON THE BRAIN'S LANGUAGE, SO WHEN WE SEE A ZIP OR ZAP WE DON'T KNOW WHAT THE IT ACTUALLY MEANS.
WHAT I'M GOING TO DO, THOMAS, IS RECORD THE SIGNATURES FROM YOUR DREAMS AND THEN FORCE-FEED THEM INTO THE SECTION OF YOUR BRAIN THAT TYPICALLY HOLDS MEMORY.
I CAN'T ACTUALLY ISOLATE ANY PARTICULAR MEMORIES, BUT I HOPE I CAN WAKE YOU UP REMEMBERING MORE THAN WHEN YOU FEEL ASLEEP.
I'M HELPING YOU REMEMBER YOUR DREAMS.
SOON...
MR. GRANT, WE HAVE A PROBLEM WITH YOUR BOY HERE.
MEANING WHAT?
MEANING YOUR BOY'S NOT DREAMING.
HOW IS THAT POSSIBLE? DOES THAT HAPPEN?
NOT VERY OFTEN, AND NOT FOR THIS LONG. JUDGING BY THE BRAIN ACTIVITY ON THE MONITOR...I'D SAY HE'S ACTUALLY AWAKE.

FATHER! FATHER!
WHAT IS IT SAMUEL?
OH THANK ELYON, THEY'RE BACK! COME, FETCH SOME CLOTHES AND LET'S GO!
FATHER!
WAIT, SAMUEL!
FIRST, WE HONOR THE FALLEN.
THEY HAVE TAKEN THREE THOUSAND OF OUR SONS AND DAUGHTERS!
COMFORT YOUR CHILDREN, MAKER OF MEN! TAKE YOUR DAUGHTERS INTO YOUR BOSOM AND WIPE AWAY THEIR TEARS!
DELIVER YOUR SONS FROM THE EVIL THAT RAVAGES WHAT IS SACRED!
COME AND SAVE US, O' ELYON!
MY LOVE!
HEY SUNSHINE. MISS ME?
MORE THAN YOU KNOW.
COME, I NEED TO SPEAK WITH CIPHUS.

CIPHUS, IT'S THE SOUTHERN FOREST.
WE MAY LOSE IT.
JAMOUS NEEDS HELP, BUT IF THE GUARD VACATES THIS FOREST WHILE SO MANY ARE COMING FOR THE ANNUAL GATHERING–
WELL, WE WON'T CANCEL THE GATHERING. AS HIGH PRIEST I CAN PROMISE YOU THAT.
WE COULD USE THE BOMBS!
THE BOMBS?
FROM THOMAS'S DREAMS IN BANGKOK.
THE BLACK POWDER WON'T DO ANYTHING IN THE OPEN DESERT.
WE CAN SEND THREE HUNDRED MEN, NO MORE.
WHAT IS BANGKOK?
THE WORLD IN HIS DREAMS. WHEN HE DREAMS, HE BELIEVES HE GOES TO ANOTHER PLACE, THAT HE'S ACTUALLY LIVING IN THE ANCIENT HISTORIES.
HE THINKS HE CAN STOP THE VIRUS THAT LED TO THE GREAT DECEPTION IN HIS DREAM WORLD.
THIS IS WHY YOU ARE SO INTERESTED IN THE BOOK OF HISTORIES? TO SAVE A DREAM WORLD?
THE DREAMS HELPED US DEFEAT THE HORDE.
PERHAPS. IF YOU SEEK TO KNOW ABOUT THE BOOKS ASK JEREMIAH OF SOUTHERN. HE IS WISE.
JEREMIAH OF SOUTHERN, THE MAN WHO HAD ONCE BEEN A SCAB?
THERE IS ANOTHER MATTER MORE PRESSING THAN DREAMS, THOMAS.
JUSTIN?
HE IS BETRAYING US ALL WITH HIS TALK. MORE FOLLOW HIM EACH DAY FURTHER HIS HERESY.
WHAT DO YOU SUGGEST?
A MEETING OF THE COUNCIL. MANY ARE ALREADY ON THEIR WAY.

THE SOUTHERN FOREST.
THEY SET FIRE TO THE FOREST AFTER THREE DAYS OF BATTLE.
THEY'VE NEVER DONE THAT BEFORE. BUT THEY'VE NEVER BEEN SO CLOSE, EITHER.
THEY'VE NEVER FOUGHT LIKE THIS. MORE ORGANIZED.
FLANKING MANEUVERS THEY'D NEVER USED BEFORE.
THIS IS THE WORK OF MARTYN.
JAMOUS, A RIDER APPROACHES.
MARKUS?
WHAT'S THIS?

JUSTIN.
MARKUS, TELL THIS DOG TO LEAVE OUR CAMP IF HE WISHES TO LIVE.
WE HAVE A WAR TO WAGE.
YOU ARE THE ONE THEY CALL JAMOUS.
DIDN'T YOU HEAR? YOU ARE NOT WELCOME HERE.
MARKUS, MUSTER THE MEN. MAKE SURE EVERYONE HAS BATHED.
STEPHEN, PULL OUT TWENTY ARCHERS AND MEET ME IN THE LOWER CAMP.
MARKUS!
THE HORDE WILL DESTROY YOU TODAY.
IF YOU ATTACK, THEY WILL CRUSH WHAT REMAINS OF YOUR ARMY AND SLAUGHTER MY PEOPLE.
YOUR PEOPLE? THE PEOPLE OF THIS FOREST ARE ALIVE BECAUSE OF MY ARMY!
YOU ABANDONED THE GUARD!
WHAT DO YOU KNOW OF WAR?
I WAGE A NEW KIND OF WAR.
ON WHOSE BEHALF? THE SCABS?
HOW MUCH BLOOD WILL YOU SPILL, JAMOUS?
AS MUCH AS ELYON DECIDES!
ELYON? AND WHO MADE THE SCABS IF NOT ELYON?
ARE YOU SAYING THAT ELYON DID NOT LEAD US AGAINST THE HORDE?

I'M SAYING THAT THE HORDE LURKS IN ALL OF US. THE DISEASE.
THE ONLY CURE FOR THE HORDE IS DEATH.
IS IT? I CAN TURN THE HORDE BACK THIS DAY BY MYSELF AND AVOID ANY MORE BLOODSHED.
THAT'S THE MOST ARROGANT THING I'VE EVER HEARD!
IF I CAN RID YOU OF THIS HORDE ARMY ON MY OWN, YOU MUST RIDE WITH ME IN VICTORY MARCH THROUGH THE ELYON VALLEY EAST OF THE VILLAGE.
AGREED?
AGREED.
LATER.
WATCH OUR FLANK! KEEP THEM TO THE FRONT!
BACK! *BACK!*
PULL BACK TO THE FOREST!

CENTER LINE! CENTER LINE!
THEY'RE CUTTING US OFF!
JAMOUS!
TURN AND ASSEMBLE!
THERE'S ONLY ONE WAY.
RIGHT. ELYON'S STRENGTH.
STRAIGHT AT THEM.
YOU'RE A GOOD MAN, JAMOUS.
AND YOU, MARKUS. I'LL SEE YOU ON THE OTHER SIDE.
RIDER BEHIND!
WHAT'S HE---

I REQUEST TO SPEAK WITH THE GENERAL NAMED MARTYN!
WHAT DOES HE THINK HE'S DOING? SURRENDERING?
I DON'T KNOW MARKUS, BUT WE ARE STILL ALIVE. FOR NOW.
WE CAN'T SURRENDER! THE HORDE TAKES NO PRISONERS!
I THINK...HE AIMS TO MAKE PEACE.
LET'S SEE IF THEY LET HIM THROUGH.
THEY'RE STOPPING HIM.
THEY'RE LETTING HIM PASS!
WHAT IS HE TELLING THEM?
HOLD YOUR TONGUE, MARKUS. IF WE LIVE TO FIGHT ANOTHER DAY, WE WILL DRAG HIM BEFORE THE FOREST COUNCIL TO STAND TRIAL FOR TREASON.

NOW WHAT, JAMOUS?
NOW, MARKUS...
...WE RIDE.

HE'S STILL SLEEPING?
CAN YOU UNLOCK THESE DREAMS OF HIS?
HE'S BEEN SLEEPING THREE HOURS AND NOT DREAMING?
IF HE IS DREAMING, IT'S NOT LIKE ANY DREAM I'VE EVER SEEN.
AS FAR AS I CAN DETECT THERE IS NOTHING THERE TO UNLOCK. I'VE NEVER SEEN ANYTHING LIKE IT...
WHATEVER IS GOING ON IN THAT MIND OF HIS IS HIGHLY IRREGULAR.
NO RAPID EYE MOVEMENT. NO PERCEPTUAL BRAIN ACTIVITY, FLUCTUATION IN BRAIN TEMPERATURE.
HE LOOKS SO... ORDINARY.
HE IS FAR FROM ORDINARY.
WAKE HIM UP.
WAKE UP, LAD.
UNNNH... HOW LONG WAS I ASLEEP?
THREE HOURS.

WHAT HAPPENED?
DID IT WORK?
DID YOU RECORD MY DREAMS?
DID YOU DREAM?
I MET WITH THE COUNCIL, AND THEN FELL ASLEEP AFTER JOINING THE CELEBRATION WITH RACHELLE.
YES. I RETURNED TO THE FOREST WITH MY ARMY AFTER DESTROYING THE HORDE. THE BLACK POWDER WAS A HIT.
IT COUL BE WORS
AND I ASKED ABOUT THE BOOKS OF HISTORIES.
I KNOW THE MAN WHO MAY BE ABLE TO TELL ME WHERE TO FIND THEM!
BUT YOU DON'T REMEMBER ANYTHING MORE ABOUT THE ANTIVIRUS.
NO. YOUR LITTLE EXPERIMENT FAILED, REMEMBER? YOU CAN'T STIMULATE MY MEMORY BANKS BECAUSE YOU CAN'T RECORD THE BRAIN SIGNATURES ASSOCIATED WITH MY DREAMS...
...BECAUSE I'M NOT DREAMING.
PERHAPS, YES!
FASCINATING. WE COULD BE ON A WHOLE NEW VERGE OF UNDERSTANDING HERE.
IT COULD BE WORSE
WHAT ABOUT THE SEARCH FOR MONIQUE?
WE'RE WORKING. THE GOVERNMENTS OF BRITAIN, GERMANY, FRANCE, THAILAND...
IT COUL BE WO
NO STRES
WE MUST FIND HER. I THINK THERE'S A CONNECTION BETWEEN RACHELLE AND MONIQUE.
WHAT? HOW?

I DON'T KNOW HOW YET, BUT SOMEHOW, THERE'S A CONNECTION BETWEEN RACHELLE AND MONIQUE.
BETWEEN BOTH WORLDS.
KNOCK! KNOCK!
WE HAVE A WAGER.
WHAT?
A WAGER. A BET.
WHO WILL FIND IT FIRST, YOU OR US.
I AM THE ONLY ONE BETTING ON YOU. YOU'VE MADE SOME GOOD PROGRESS OVER THE LAST FEW DAYS...
NONE OF US WILL FIND IT! DON'T YOU SEE WHAT'S HAPPENING?
HE'S GOING TO RELEASE THE VIRUS, YOU FOOL!
OF COURSE I DO! THE FIRST TO ISOLATE THE ANTIVIRUS WILL BE PAID FIFTY MILLION DOLLARS!
NOT GOING TO. HE ALREADY HAS.

SLAM!
NO, WAIT!
YOU'RE LYING! THERE'S NO WAY TO KNOW IF AN ANTIVIRUS EVEN EXISTS! HE'D BE CRAZY TO...
YOU HAVE TO FOCUS, MONIQUE.
FATHER WILL HAVE THE WHOLE WORLD LOOKING FOR YOU. THEY WILL FIND YOU.
NO...
THIS CAN'T BE RIGHT!
I'M AFRAID IT IS.

SORRY TO LEAVE YOU ALONE FOR SO LONG, BUT I'VE HAD A FEW THINGS THAT HAVE REQUIRED MY ATTENTION.
THE LAST COUPLE DAYS HAVE BEEN QUITE EVENTFUL.
WHAT'S GOING ON? WHERE ARE WE?
YOU HAVE NO IDEA HOW EXCITING THE WORLD HAS BECOME IN THE LAST 48 HOURS, BECAUSE YOU'VE BEEN HARD AT WORK TRYING TO SAVE IT.
WE'RE ON AN INDONESIAN ISLAND, INSIDE A MOUNTAIN CALLED CYCLOPS.
YOU'LL BE CALLING THIS HOME FOR A FEW MORE DAYS.
HAVE YOU MADE ANY PROGRESS?
WITH WHAT? YOU'VE GIVEN ME AN IMPOSSIBLE TASK.
THEN YOU'RE NOT AS MOTIVATED AS I'D HOPED.
PLEASE INSERT THIS DISK.
I'M SURE YOU WILL FIND THIS OF GREAT INTEREST.

THIS IS A SIMULATION. ANYONE CAN CREATE A CARTOON, SVENSSON.
I ASSURE YOU, NOT A SINGLE PIECE OF HYPOTHETICAL DATA HAS BEEN USED FOR THIS...CARTOON, AS YOU CALL IT.
I'LL LEAVE IT FOR YOU TO ANALYZE LATER.
NASTY LITTLE BEAST.
LIKE AN AWAKENED DRAGON.
THAT WAS OUR INITIAL DEPOSIT...
1DAY
FROM THERE, NATURE DID THE REST.
SO, NOW YOU ARE FULLY UP TO DATE.
2DAY
3DAY
YOU'RE SAYING YOU'VE ACTUALLY DONE IT?
WE'VE DONE IT.

WE CALCULATE THAT IT WILL TAKE TWO WEEKS FOR THE VIRUS TO INFECT OVER 90% OF THE WORLD'S POPULATION.
ODORLESS.
I SEE YOU NEED MORE CONVINCING.
BRING HIM DOWN.
THIS IS CRAZY! THE UNITED STATES WOULD COME UNGLUED IF--
THE UNITED STATES *IS* COMING UNGLUED!
EVERY NATION WITH ANYTHING RESEMBLING A GOVERNMENT IS COMING UNGLUED.
THE CDC HAS VERIFIED THE VIRUS'S PRESENCE IN MORE THAN FIFTY US CITIES AND COUNTING.
LOOK FOR YOURSELF, MS. DE RAISON.
PERHAPS YOU'LL BELIEVE ME WHEN YOU SEE THE VIRUS FOR YOURSELF.

WE PICKED HIM UP IN A PARIS NIGHTCLUB.
WE DON'T EVEN KNOW HIS NAME, BUT HIS CHANCES OF INFECTION ARE PRETTY GOOD, CONSIDERING WHERE HE WAS SPENDING HIS TIME.
MMMPH
A LITTLE SOMETHING FOR YOU TO ANALYZE.
IT CAN'T BE!
BLAM!
NO MORE GAMES, MONIQUE.
WITHOUT AN ANTIVIRUS WE ALL WILL DIE.

WE KNOW THAT YOU ALWAYS ENGINEER A BACK DOOR INTO YOUR VACCINES. WE NEED YOU TO SHOW US THIS BACK DOOR, AND VERIFY THAT IT HASN'T MUTATED WITH THE VACCINE---
--AND THEN CREATE AN ANTIVIRUS THAT WILL SHUT THE RAISON STRAIN DOWN.
SO, YOU RELEASE A DEADLY VIRUS, THEN PLAN TO BE THE ONLY ONE IN THE WORLD WITH THE ANTIVIRUS. IT'S ABOUT MONEY?
IS IT?
YOU HAVE A LOT OF WORK TO DO, SO WE SHOULD BE LEAVING.
BILLIONS OF LIVES ARE AT STAKE HERE. BILLIONS.
YOU DON'T KNOW WHAT YOU'VE DONE.
OH, WE DO.
WE?
AND I, LIKE YOU, AM ONLY PLAYING MY PART. EVERYONE MUST PLAY THEIR PART OR THIS GAME WILL INDEED END BADLY.
NOW, I MUST BE GOING. YOU HAVE A WORLD TO SAVE.

PARIS. INSIDE THE CHATEAU TRIOMPHE...
THIS IS AN OUTRAGE! YOU'RE FRANCE'S MINISTER OF FOREIGN AFFAIRS, NOT A TERRORIST. YOU CAN'T DO THIS FORTIER.
CAN'T? I ALREADY HAVE, PRIME MINISTER.
WHAT ARE YOU SAYING, ARMAND? THAT YOU WORK FOR VALBORG SVENNSON? THAT WE SHOULD GIVE INTO HIS DEMANDS? IS THAT IT?
NO. I'M SUGGESTING YOU GIVE INTO MY DEMANDS.
SO HE WORKS FOR YOU.
GENTLEMEN, I'LL MAKE THIS CLEAR. THE RAISON STRAIN IS GROWING INSIDE MILLIONS OF PEOPLE WORLDWIDE AS WE SPEAK.
WHAT THOSE POOR PEOPLE DON'T KNOW IS AN ANTIVIRUS EXISTS.
AND I CONTROL IT.
VERY FEW MEN IN THIS WORLD WILL BE GIVEN THE KIND OF OPPORTUNITY I'M GIVING YOU TONIGHT. IT WON'T BE OFFERED TWICE.
MAY I ASK A FEW QUESTIONS, ARMAND?
PLEASE.
NO! THIS IS MORALLY REPREHENSIBLE! FRANCE WILL NOT BE A PART OF THIS. WE CANNOT HOLD THE WORLD HOSTAGE.
BESIDES, THE SUPERPOWERS WON'T JUST FLOAT THEIR NUCLEAR ARSENALS TO FRANCE BECAUSE WE DEMAND IT. THEY'LL LAUNCH THEM FIRST!

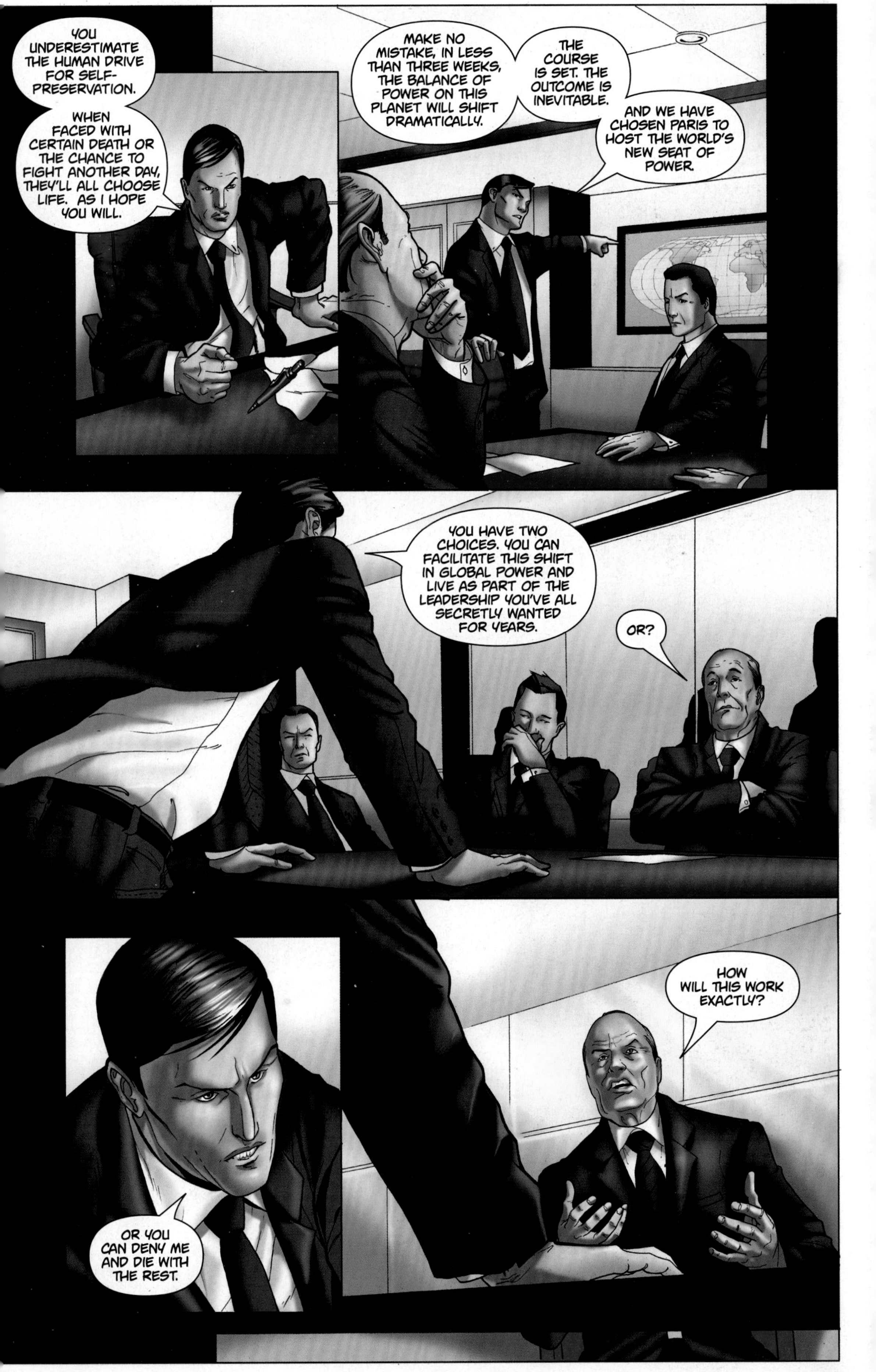
YOU UNDERESTIMATE THE HUMAN DRIVE FOR SELF-PRESERVATION.
WHEN FACED WITH CERTAIN DEATH OR THE CHANCE TO FIGHT ANOTHER DAY, THEY'LL ALL CHOOSE LIFE. AS I HOPE YOU WILL.
MAKE NO MISTAKE, IN LESS THAN THREE WEEKS, THE BALANCE OF POWER ON THIS PLANET WILL SHIFT DRAMATICALLY.
THE COURSE IS SET. THE OUTCOME IS INEVITABLE.
AND WE HAVE CHOSEN PARIS TO HOST THE WORLD'S NEW SEAT OF POWER.
YOU HAVE TWO CHOICES. YOU CAN FACILITATE THIS SHIFT IN GLOBAL POWER AND LIVE AS PART OF THE LEADERSHIP YOU'VE ALL SECRETLY WANTED FOR YEARS.
OR?
OR YOU CAN DENY ME AND DIE WITH THE REST.
HOW WILL THIS WORK EXACTLY?

AN HOUR LATER...
...THE UNITED STATES WILL HAVE TO TAKE EXTRAORDINARY MEASURES TO SHIP ALL THEIR NUCLEAR WEAPONS HERE, BUT WE ARE DEMANDING NOTHING OF THEM OR ANYONE ELSE THAT CAN'T BE DONE.
AS FOR THE BRITISH, INDIA, PAKISTAN AND ISRAEL, WE ARE DEMANDING THEIR ENTIRE NUCLEAR ARSENAL.
IN EXCHANGE FOR ANTIVIRUS?
YES.
ANY MORE QUESTIONS?
I'VE HEARD ENOUGH.
I CAN'T LET THIS HAPPEN. WE WON'T LET THIS HAPPEN. I CAN ASSURE YOU OF THAT.
IS THAT SO, OLD FRIEND? THEN MAYBE IT'S TIME FOR SOMEONE ELSE TO LEAD OUR BELOVED COUNTRY.
SOMEONE WHO CAN MAKE THE TOUGH DECISIONS.
LET ME SHOW YOU AN EXAMPLE OF HOW THIS IS GOING TO PLAY OUT, GENTLEMAN.
JEAN, WOULD YOU ASSIST ME, PLEASE?
BLAM!
WE ALL DIE IN 18 DAYS UNLESS WE DO EXACTLY WHAT I HAVE SAID.
IF ANYONE ELSE DOUBTS ME, LET HIM SPEAK NOW.
NOW IS THE TIME FOR STRENGTH GENTLEMEN. IT'S TIME TO FULFILL OUR DESTINY.

BLOOD? WAS RACHELLE BLEEDING?
YES, A SMALL CUT ON HER ARM. I HADN'T NOTICED THAT YESTERDAY ON HER.
BUT WAS ALL THIS BLOOD FROM THAT?
OF COURSE. I'D CUT MYSELF IN BANCROFT'S LAB.
I'D BEEN SLEEPING HERE WHEN THAT HAPPENED, AND I BLED HERE, EXACTLY AS I THOUGHT MIGHT HAPPEN.
MY FOREARM HAD RUBBED RACHELLE'S ARM. SO THE BLOOD WAS HALF MINE, HALF HERS...
I NEED TO STOP THE VIRUS! IF I CAN'T I WILL DIE IN THE OTHER REALITY- WHICH MEANS THEY WOULD ALL DIE!
I NEED TO FIND JEREMIAH OF SOUTHERN. HE WON'T BE HAPPY TO BE WOKEN AT THIS HOUR, BUT THERE'S NO TIME.
CIPHUS SAID HE WAS STAYING AT THE GUESTHOUSE THAT ANASTASIA OVERSEES.

WHO IS IT?
THOMAS OF HUNTER.
THOMAS? THOMAS OF HUNTER? COME IN, COME IN.
HERE, THOMAS, SIT ON MY BED. LET ME GET US A DRINK.
NO, NO. SIT DOWN PLEASE. I HAVE AN URGENT QUESTION.
HOW CAN I HAVE SUCH AN HONORED GUEST HERE AND NOT OFFER HIM A DRINK?
I CAME ABOUT THE BOOKS OF HISTORIES.
I SEE.
WHERE ARE THEY?
IT'S POSSIBLE THEY ARE WITH THE HORDE. I'VE NEVER ACTUALLY SEEN THEM.
BUT I'VE HEARD IT SAID THAT THE BOOKS FOLLOW QURONG INTO BATTLE.
CAN QURONG READ THEM?
I DON'T THINK SO. I'M NOT SURE *YOU* COULD READ THEM.
BUT SURELY SOMEONE CAN READ THEM. COULD YOU?
ME? I DON'T KNOW. THEY MAY NOT EVEN EXIST.

THE BOOKS OF HISTORIES HAD LONG AGO BEEN TAKEN FROM ELYON'S PEOPLE AND COMMITTED TO AN ORAL HISTORY.
TANIS HIMSELF HAD BEEN LED DOWN THE WRONG PATH BY HIS FASCINATION WITH THEIR WISDOM. THAT TYPE OF KNOWLEDGE HELD GREAT POWER.
PERHAPS THE MAN WAS RIGHT. PERHAPS THE BOOKS WERE NOT MEANT FOR MAN.
BUT I NEED THEM.
I'M GOING AFTER THEM, JEREMIAH.
THAT WOULD MEAN FACING QURONG HIMSELF!
PERHAPS WE CAN FIND A MORE SUBTLE APPROACH.
YOU WILL STILL NEED TO FIND HIM.
I WOULD WAGER THAT QURONG IS WITH THE ARMY WE DEFEATED IN THE NATALGA GAP. THEY'RE IN THE DESERT WEST OF HERE, LICKING THEIR WOUNDS.
THE COMMANDER'S TENT ALWAYS LIES IN THE CENTER OF THEIR CAMP, ISN'T THAT RIGHT?
YES BUT SURROUNDED BY HIS ARMY, YOU'D HAVE TO BE ONE OF THEM TO GET ANYWHERE NEAR THEM!
WHY RISK THE LIFE OF OUR GREATEST WARRIOR FOR A FEW OLD BOOKS THAT MAY NOT EVEN EXIST?
BECAUSE IF I DON'T FIND THEM, I'M ALREADY DEAD.
WE ALL MIGHT BE.

WHERE AM I?
WHO AM I?
MONIQUE DE RAISON...
MY NAME IS...
MOTHER! MOTHER! WAKE UP! WHERE IS FATHER?
THOMAS?
HE'S NOT HERE! DID HE GO OUT ON PATROLS?
NO...HE SHOULD BE HERE.
WELL, HIS ARMOR'S GONE, AND HIS SWORD.
I ASKED IN THE VILLAGE. NO ONE KNOWS WHERE HE IS.

THE LABORATORY!
I'VE ENTERED THOMAS'S DREAM WORLD!
I MUST TELL THOMAS!
BUT WHERE IS HE? CIPHUS WILL KNOW.
LATER...
WHERE? ON PATROL?
YES. IT'S A... PATROL.
STOP BEING SO EVASIVE. HE WOULD HAVE TOLD ME IF IT WERE A PATROL.
HE'S GONE AFTER THE BOOKS, HASN'T HE, JEREMIAH, HASN'T HE? YOU TOLD HIM WHERE HE MIGHT FIND THE BOOKS AND HE'S GONE AFTER HIM!
I'M SORRY RACHELLE, HE INSISTED...
I BEG YOU CHILD, DON'T GO AFTER HIM!
HE MEANS TO BECOME ONE OF THEM... TO ENTER THEIR CAMP!
I KNEW IT! I HAVE TO FIND THOMAS! I MUST TELL HIM ABOUT MY CONNECTION WITH MONIQUE.
BEFORE IT'S TOO LATE.

THE NATALGA GAP.
ARRGHH, THE STENCH...
HARD TO BELIEVE WE DID ALL OF THIS.
DON'T THINK FOR A MOMENT THAT WE'VE SEEN THE LAST OF THEM. THEY'LL REGROUP AND RETURN. WITH FAR GREATER NUMBERS.
IT WAS SAID THAT THE HORDE CARED LESS FOR THE LIVES OF THEIR OWN MEN THAN THE LIVES OF THEIR HORSES.
ANY SCAB THAT DEFIED HIS LEADER WAS PUNISHED WITHOUT TRIAL.
IT WASN'T UNUSUAL TO FIND A SCAB SOLDIER WITH NUMEROUS BONES BROKEN LEFT TO DIE ON THE HOT DESERT SAND WITHOUT HAVING SHED A DROP OF BLOOD. PUNISHMENT.
PUBLIC EXECUTIONS INVOLVED DROWNING THE OFFENDER, A PROSPECT THAT INSTILLED MORE FEAR FOR THE SCABS THAN ANY OTHER THREAT OF DEATH.
LET'S GO, ALL OF YOU.
DRESS.
I NEVER WOULD HAVE THOUGHT WE'D HAVE TO STOOP SO LOW AS TO DRESS IN THESE MAGGOTS' CLOTHES. NEVER.

THEY'RE LEARNING.
THEIR TECHNOLOGY ISN'T THAT FAR BEHIND OUR OWN.
THEY DON'T HAVE BLACK POWDER.
I'LL HAVE DEFENSES BUILT AROUND EVERY FOREST IN 3 MONTHS. THEY WON'T STAND A CHANCE.
UNTIL THEY TOO HAVE BLACK POWDER. IF THEY HAD EXPLOSIVES, CAN YOU IMAGINE WHAT THEY COULD DO TO OUR FORESTS?
THEY'RE GROWING BRAVER AND SMARTER, AND WE'RE RUNNING OUT OF WARRIORS.
SO WHAT WOULD YOU SUGGEST? TREASON?
LIKE JUSTIN?
HE DEFEATED THE HORDE WITHOUT ONE SWIPE OF HIS BLADE.
THERE WERE WHISPERS; SOME CALLED HIM A PROPHET.
TRAITOR.
HAVE I EVER SUGGESTED YIELDING TO THE HORDE IN ANY WAY?
YOU HAVE NO NEED TO QUESTION MY LOYALTY MIKIL.
YOU'RE RIGHT, I MEANT NO DISRESPECT.
PULL UP YOUR HOODS.
FROM HERE ON WE RIDE IN SILENCE.
IGNORE THE PAIN OF THE DISEASE. WHEN IT COMES.

THAT'S SOME CAMP.
THERE'S QURONG'S TENT IN THE CENTER. IT MUST BE A GOOD HALF-MILE FROM HERE.
WITH A LOT OF HORDE IN BETWEEN.
LET'S GO.
REMEMBER, DON'T SPEAK UNLESS DIRECTLY QUESTIONED. AVOID EYE CONTACT.
AND WALK SLOWLY, WILLIAM, LIKE YOU HAVE THE PAIN.
I DO HAVE THE PAIN, THOMAS. MY SKIN IS ALREADY ITCHING. HOW LONG BEFORE THIS AFFECTS OUR MIND?
IF WE GET OUT BY MORNING WE'LL BE FINE.
TORVIL, YOU UNGRACIOUS PIECE OF MEAT!
YOUR BROTHER IS DYING IN HERE AND YOU'RE OFF LOOKING FOR WOMEN WHERE THERE ARE NONE?
I...
ANSWER ME!
YOU'RE AS BLIND AS THE BATS THAT CURSED YOU! AM I TORVIL?
I WOULD BE LUCKY TO FIND A WOMAN IN THIS STINKING PLACE.
BAH!
ARE YOU MAD?
IT'S HOW THEY WOULD SPEAK. I THINK...
WHAT DO YOU THINK?
WE'LL GO IN THE SIDE AND SEE WHAT WE CAN LEARN.

NO! WILLIAM, SHE CAN HELP US.
MAKE ONE SOUND AND I'LL SLIT YOUR THROAT.
WE'RE NOT HERE TO KILL YOU, BUT WE WILL IF WE HAVE TO.
UNDERSTAND?
MMMPH
THE BOOKS OF HISTORIES. ARE THEY IN ANY OF THESE TENTS?
I WILL BE DROWNED FOR TELLING YOU! PLEASE I BEG YOU!
TELL ME WHERE THEY ARE AND I WILL MAKE IT APPEAR YOU WERE ASSAULTED. NO HARM WILL COME TO YOU.
I AM A MAN OF MY WORD.
THEY ARE IN THE GREAT ONE'S BEDCHAMBER! IN THE SECOND TENT."
ARE THERE GUARDS?
I DON'T KNOW, I SWEAR.
WILLIAM STAY HERE WITH HER, I WILL GO ALONE.
IF I DON'T RETURN IN HALF AN HOUR, GET OUT.

A DRINK, GENERAL?
WHY NOT?
IT'S BEEN A GOOD DAY, A GOOD DAY INDEED.
AND THIS IS ONLY THE BEGINNING!
GENERAL. IT MUST BE MARTYN.
THE BRILLIANCE OF THE PLAN IS ITS BOLDNESS. THEY MAY SUSPECT, BUT WITH OUR FORCES AT THEIR DOORSTEP, THEY WILL HAVE NO CHOICE.
WE'LL SPEAK ABOUT PEACE AND THEY WILL LISTEN BECAUSE THEY MUST.
BY THE TIME WE WORK OUR BETRAYAL WITH HIM, IT WILL BE TOO LATE.
IT IS LATE AND THE PLEASURES OF MY WIFE BECKON ME. NOT A WORD TO THE REST, MY FRIEND.
BETRAYAL?
OF COURSE. HERE'S TO PEACE, MY LORD.
TO "PEACE." HA!
WHAT'S-- IS SOMEONE THERE?
NOW!
THUNK!
WELL? YOU FOUND QURONG'S BEDCHAMBER?
WE HAVE TIME. BUT THEIR MIGHTY GENERAL, MARTYN, DOES NOT.
I JUST KILLED HIM.

HE'LL BE MISSED SOON, SO WE'VE GOT TO MOVE FAST.
SSSHHKK!
ERRRRRR....
ERRRRRRR....
THE STORIES OF HISTORY...
ERRRMM....
COUGH
COUGH
TIME TO GO.
REMEMBER WILLIAM, WALK SLOWLY.
WE JUST MIGHT GET OUT OF HERE ALIVE.

THE BOOK...
IT'S BLANK!
NOT A SINGLE MARK ON ANY OF THE PAGES. THIS WAS THE FIRST ONE I PICKED UP, BUT THERE'S NOTHING HERE!
WE NEED TO GET SOME OF THE OTHERS.
IT'S TOO RISKY NOW. WE'LL WAIT AND GO IN TOMORROW NIGHT.
YOU CAN'T LAST UNTIL TOMORROW NIGHT!
ANOTHER DAY AND YOU'LL LOSE YOUR MIND TO THE DISEASE!
THEN I'LL BATHE AND PUT ON ASH AND SNEAK BACK IN...OR--
THOMAS!
RACHELLE? WHAT ARE YOU DOING HERE?
THOMAS, THANK ELYON!
ARE YOU OK?
YES... WE HAD TO GO IN DRESSED LIKE ONE OF THEM. I HAVEN'T BATHED.
IT'S DANGEROUS FOR YOU TO BE HERE.
HOW COULD YOU DO THIS WITHOUT TELLING ME?
YOU HAVEN'T BATHED? HAVE YOU GONE MAD?
WASH. HURRY. WE NEED TO TALK.
ALONE.

I'M SORRY, LOVE. I HAD TO COME AND I COULDN'T WORRY YOU.
RUNNING OFF WOULDN'T WORRY ME?
I'M SORRY. I JUST...
DON'T EVER DO THAT AGAIN! I KNOW WHAT YOU WERE TRYING TO DO.
YOU KNEW I CAME FOR THE BOOKS?
I TALKED TO JEREMIAH. AND I'M GUESSING YOU DIDN'T TAKE THE FRUIT LAST NIGHT... AS WE AGREED YOU WOULD.
I HAD TO DREAM.
I DREAMED LAST NIGHT TOO...
...OF THE HISTORIES.
YOU'RE SURE?
SURE ENOUGH TO CHASE YOU ACROSS THE DESERT.
SURE ENOUGH TO CHASE YOU ACROSS THE DESERT.
HOW IS THAT POSSIBLE? MAYBE YOU DREAMED OF SOMETHING THAT FELT LIKE THE HISTORIES.
I WAS I A PLACE CALLED A LAB, WORKING ON SOMETHING CALLED THE RAISON STRAIN.
NOT ONLY WAS I THERE, BUT I HAD A NAME. I SHARED THE MIND OF A WOMAN NAMED...
MONIQUE.
YOU... HOW'S THAT POSSIBLE? YOU WERE... THERE?
STOP ASKING ME THAT! I DON'T KNOW HOW IT'S POSSIBLE. NONE OF IT MAKES SENSE TO ME, ANY MORE THAN IT EVER MADE SENSE TO YOU.

I WOKE UP AND MY FINGER WAS CUT. BUT IT HAPPENED IN MY DREAM.
NO, THOMAS. I REMEMBER IT CLEARLY. BEFORE I SAW MONIQUE'S FACE, SHE HANDLED SOME PARCHMENT THAT CUT HER FINGER.
MAYBE YOU IMAGINED YOU WERE CUTTING YOURSELF THERE, WORKING ON THE VIRUS I'VE SPOKEN OF MANY TIMES?
THOMAS, YOU HAVE TO BELIEVE ME! I SAW...THE COMPUTER OR A...A MICRO... SOMETHING.
THERE WAS A DEVICE THAT LOOKS INTO VERY SMALL THINGS. HOW COULD I KNOW THAT?
WE NEVER SPOKE OF THESE THINGS. YOU NEED TO BELIEVE ME LIKE I BELIEVED YOU.
I DO BELIEVE YOU, BUT...I'M THOMAS IN BOTH REALITIES, AND I LOOK THE SAME IN BOTH. YOU DON'T LOOK LIKE MONIQUE.
DO YOU KNOW, IS MONIQUE SLEEPING NOW?
I DON'T THINK SHE KNOWS ABOUT ME.
PERHAPS BECAUSE SHE HASN'T DREAMED OF YOU!
I HAVE TO GET THE OTHER BOOKS OF HISTORIES BEFORE THE HORDE MOVES!
NO. YOU MUST DREAM.
THERE ISN'T TIME.
BUT, THOMAS...
I THINK I KNOW WHERE MONIQUE IS BEING HELD.

WASHINGTON, D.C.
YOU'RE SURE ABOUT THIS, THOMAS?
YOU KNOW MONIQUE'S DE RAISON'S LOCATION?
YES SIR. BUT WE NEED TO MOVE QUICKLY. SHE MAY NOT BE THERE FOR LONG.
THOMAS, FIVE OF THE FRENCH LEADERS WERE SEEN IN AN UNSCHEDULED MEETING YESTERDAY. ONLY FOUR CAME OUT.
A COUP?
MAYBE NOT A COUP, BUT THE FRENCH MAY BE CONNECTED TO SVENSSON.
BAD NEWS, GENTLEMAN. WE HAVE TWENTY-FOUR HOURS TO SHOW MOVEMENT OF OUR ARMS. WE'RE SUPPOSED TO MOVE THEM TO THE BREST NAVAL BASE IN NORTHERN FRANCE.
THE FRENCH CLAIM THEY ARE COOPERATING BECAUSE THEY HAVE TO.
THEY'RE LYING.
RON?
HE'S PROBABLY RIGHT, SIR. EITHER WAY, IT DOESN'T MATTER. EVEN IF SVENSSON IS HOLDING HANDS WITH THE FRENCH, WE CAN'T VERY WELL DROP NUKES ON PARIS.
THE CLOCK IS TICKING, THOMAS.
SO, IT'S TIME FOR THESE DREAMS OF YOURS TO DELIVER.
YES SIR.
A CIA INSERTION TEAM IS GEARING UP AS WE SPEAK. I'VE AUTHORIZED THEM TO DO WHATEVER IS NECESSARY.
FIND MONIQUE DE RAISON.
LET'S PRAY YOU ARE RIGHT ABOUT HER LOCATION, SON. IT'S A LONG FLIGHT TO INDONESIA, SO BE SURE TO GET SOME SLEEP.

WOREF, WHO DID THIS?
THE FOREST GUARD, SIRE.
HOW? HOW DID THIS HAPPEN?
WE'VE TAKEN A CONFESSION FROM ONE OF THE SERVANTS. TWO OF THEM BROKE IN AND CAME FOR THE BOOKS OF HISTORIES.
DROWN THE GUARD THAT WAS ON WATCH, AND BRING ME THE CHEST.
I FOUND THIS IN YOUR TENT, SIRE. THE LEATHER WAS CUT.
THEY WERE IN MY TENT!
IT SEEMS THEY WERE ONLY AFTER THE BOOKS.
SEND MEN IMMEDIATELY. CUT OFF ANY FOREST GUARD THAT IS NEARBY.
I SWEAR, WOREF, IF THOMAS OF HUNTER IS AMONG THEM, HE WILL NOT LIVE OUT THIS DAY.
WAKE UP. THEY'RE MOVING.
SIR...
THERE'S MOVEMENT IN THEIR CAMP. THEY'RE ONTO US.
READY THE HORSES AND TELL THE OTHERS.
WE CAN OUTRUN THEM, BUT ONLY IF WE LEAVE NOW.

THEY'RE CUTTING US OFF! BACK!
SOUTH!
THERE'S NO WAY TO FIGHT OUR WAY OUT.
WELL DONE, QURONG.

OF COURSE.
THE BOOK.
THE BOOKS OF HISTORIES! I HAVE A BOOK OF HISTORY!
I HAVE A BOOK!
IT'S NOT WORKING.
STEADY, WE CAN TAKE THESE.
THERE ARE TOO MANY!
STEADY! IT'S OUR ONLY CHANCE!

I AM THOMAS OF HUNTER, AND I HAVE THE BOOKS OF HISTORIES, WHICH YOUR LEADER QURONG REVERES!
I DARE ANY MAN TO TEST MY POWERS!
PERRRRPPUUU!
SIR, ON THE RIDGE!
PERRRRPPUUU!
JUSTIN?

HELLO, THOMAS.
IT'S BEEN AWHILE.
TWO YEARS.
YES, TWO YEARS. YOU LOOK WELL, MY FRIEND.
ACTUALLY, I COULD USE A SWIM IN THE LAKE.
COULDN'T WE ALL?
INCLUDING THESE...FRIENDS OF YOURS?
ESPECIALLY THEM. NEVER CAN GET USED TO THE SMELL.
THE SMELL MIGHT BE COMING FROM YOUR SKIN AS WELL AS THEIRS.
YOU SEEM TO HAVE GOTTEN YOURSELF IN SOME TROUBLE HERE.
PERCEPTIVE.
WE DON'T NEED YOUR HELP, JUSTIN.
MIKIL!
HAVE YOU, BY CHANCE, NOTICED HOW LARGE THE HORDE'S ARMIES ARE THESE DAYS?
WE'VE ALWAYS BEEN OUT NUMBERED.
TRUE, BUT THIS ISN'T A WAR YOU CAN WIN, THOMAS.
NOT THIS WAY.
NOT WITH THE SWORD.

THEN HOW WOULD YOU SUGGEST WE FIGHT?
WITH A SMILE AND A HANDSHAKE?
NO, THOMAS.
WITH LOVE.
WE DO LOVE. WE LOVE OUR WIVES AND CHILDREN BY SENDING THESE MONSTERS TO HELL WHERE THEY CAME FROM.
I WASN'T AWARE THEY CAME FROM HELL.
I WAS ALWAYS UNDER THE IMPRESSION THEY WERE CREATED BY ELYON. LIKE YOU.
AND SO WERE THE SHATAIKI. SHOULD WE BEFRIEND THEM AS WELL?
MOST OF YOU ALREADY HAVE.
I FEAR THE BATS HAVE LEFT THE TREES TO MAKE THEIR HOME IN YOUR HEARTS.
SIR, I CAN'T SIT HERE AND LISTEN TO THIS POISON.
YOU KNOW IT'S TRUE, DON'T YOU THOMAS?
I CAN SEE IT IN YOUR EYES.

MIKIL HAS A POINT. DID YOU COME HERE TO HELP OR ARE YOU MORE INTERESTED IN CONVERTING US TO YOUR NEW RELIGION?
RELIGION? THE PROBLEM WITH THE GREAT ROMANCE IS IT'S BECOME A RELIGION.
I AM HERE TO SHOW YOU A NEW WAY. A WAY BACK TO THE GREAT ROMANCE, AS ELYON MEANT IT.
ME, THOMAS. I'M THE WAY. LISTEN TO WHAT I SAY...
NO, YOU'VE SAID ENOUGH. HELP...OR LEAVE.
AH, A BOOK OF HISTORY. THE POWER TO CREATE AND TO DESTROY.
WHATEVER YOU DO, DON'T LOSE IT. IN THE WRONG HANDS IT CAN CAUSE TROUBLE.
TRUST ME, MY FRIEND, SOON YOU WILL SEE.
BUT IT'S EMPTY.
BE WELL, THOMAS. I'LL SEE YOU AT THE GATHERING.
PERRRRPPUUU!
DID YOU HEAR THAT BLASPHEMY? I COULD KILL THAT---
SILENCE. NOT ANOTHER WORD, MIKIL.
THEY'RE... LEAVING.
BE THANKFUL. OUR LIVES HAVE BEEN SPARED.
YES. BUT, AT WHAT COST, THOMAS?

SOMEWHERE OVER CYCLOPS ISLAND. INDONESIA.
NOTHING YET.
YOU SURE WE SHOULDN'T COVER THE OTHER SIDE?
NO, THIS SIDE. I'M SURE OF IT.
YOU KNOW ANYONE DOWN THERE IS GOING TO HEAR US. THIS THING'S A FLYING STAMPEDE.
YOU HAVE AN ALTERNATIVE?
NO, BUT I GOTTA TELL YOU, IF THEY'RE DOWN THERE, THEY'RE ALL EYES.
I'M NOT SURE WE DON'T WANT THEM TO FIND US, CAPTAIN. IF WE'RE LUCKY, WE'LL FORCE THEIR HAND.
IF YOU SAY SO THOMAS. BUT WE'RE HANGING OUR REAR ENDS OUT PRETTY FAR.
I REALIZE THAT, CAPTAIN.
SO LET'S TAKE HER DOWN.

THEY'RE COMING IN LOWER NOW.
HOW MANY TIMES IS THAT NOW?
THIS WILL BE THEIR THIRD SWEEP.
HOW DID THEY FIND US?
HE KNEW ABOUT THE VIRUS, THE ANTIVIRUS, NOW WHERE WE ARE.
HE'S A GHOST.
THEN IT'S TIME TO BRING YOUR GHOST IN FOR A TALK.
YOU DON'T THINK A CRASH WILL KILL HIM?
I DON'T. THE REST MAYBE, BUT NOT HUNTER.
THEN BRING THEM DOWN. NO SURVIVORS.
AND OUR DEPARTURE?
TONIGHT. FORTIER WANTS THIS MAN IN FRANCE.

CONTACT BEARING, TWO-NINE-ZERO...
CONTACT... INCOMING! INCOMING!
COUNTER-MEASURES DEPLOYED!
IT'S GONNA HIT! IT'S GONNA HIT!
HANG ON!
WHUMP!
BOOM!

LATER.
I'M ALIVE.
OH NO.
I'VE GOT TO GET TO THEM!
SLOW DOWN, SLOW DOWN. THINK!
HOPEFULLY SOME OF THE OTHERS GOT OUT.
I SEE HIM.
SOUTH.

HOW FAR?
HALF A KLICK. RUNNING UP THE RIVER.
TAKE THE SHOT?
NLY IF YOU OW YOU CAN T HIM BELOW THE NECK.
ARE OU SURE IT'S HIM?
AFFIRMATIVE.
DO IT.
STATUS?
WE HAVE HIM IN OUR SIGHTS.
SO HE DID SURVIVE.
YES. AND HEALTHY.
GOOD. KEEP HIM THAT WAY.
TARGET DOWN.
HE'S STILL DOWN?
DOWN.
MOVE QUICKLY. HE MAY NOT BE DOWN FOR LONG.

ONE HOUR LATER.
THUNK!
THOMAS!
WAKE UP... COME ON THOMAS, I NEED YOU AWAKE!
UHHH
MONIQUE...
GET UP.
THE ROOM IS SPINNING. THEY MUST'VE DRUGGED ME.

MAN, FEELS LIKE I HEAD BUTTED A TRAIN.
WAIT... I DIDN'T DREAM!
MAYBE IT WAS THE DRUGS.
IT'S THE FIRST TIME I HAVEN'T DREAMED IN TWO WEEKS. I MEAN FROM THIS SIDE, ANYWAY.
THERE I STOPPED DREAMING FOR YEARS BY TAKING THE RHAMBUTAN FRUIT.
RHAMBUTAN?
I THINK YOU MIGHT BE CONNECTED TO RACHELLE, TOO.
RACHELLE...
COME CLOSER TO ME SO THEY CAN'T HEAR US.
HOW DID YOU FIND ME?
RACHELLE FOUND YOU, IN A DREAM.
LISTEN, THE VIRUS HAS BEEN RELEASED. 24 GATEWAY AIRPORTS.
I CAN'T BELIEVE THIS HAS HAPPENED. WE TOOK EVERY PRECAUTION!
IT ISN'T YOUR FAULT.
IF ANYONE IS TO BLAME HERE, IT'S ME. I WAS THE ONE WHO TOLD THE WORLD HOW YOUR VACCINE COULD BE CHANGED INTO THE VIRUS IT'S BECOME. REMEMBER?

WHAT ABOUT MY FATHER? IS THE COMPANY LOOKING FOR A WAY?
YOUR FATHER IS SCREAMING BLOODY MURDER IN BANGKOK, BUT APART FROM TRYING TO FIND AN ANTIVIRUS, THERE'S NOT A LOT HE CAN DO.
THEY HAVE LEADS, THEN?
BESIDES YOU...NO.
YOU MEAN THE BACK DOOR.
YES, I'M GUESSING THAT'S WHY SVENSSON TOOK YOU IN THE FIRST PLACE. DID YOUR KEY SURVIVE THE MUTATION?
HOPEFULLY.
THANK ELY-GOD.
WAIT. HOPEFULLY?
WELL, I HAVEN'T TRIED IT YET. I GAVE IT TO THEM TWENTY-FOUR HOURS AGO.
CAN YOU WRITE IT DOWN FOR ME?
YES, BUT I'D RATHER YOU JUST TAKE ME OUT OF HERE. AND IT'S ALREADY WRITTEN DOWN BY THE COMPUTER.
TRUST ME, I'M NOT GOING ANYWHERE WITHOUT YOU. I'D NEVER HEAR THE END OF IT.
FROM MY FATHER?
NO. RACHELLE.

Creeeeeek!
I'LL GET THE PAPER...
PUT HIM IN THE CHAIR.
HE'S NOT GOING ANYWHERE.
SO THIS IS THE MAN WHO HAS GIVEN US BOTH THE WORLD AND A WORLD OF TROUBLE.
I MUST SAY, YOUNG MAN, YOU LOOK YOUNGER THAN YOUR PICTURES.
I HAVE SOME QUESTIONS FOR YOU MR. HUNTER, AND I'M AFRAID I HAVE TO INSIST THAT YOU ANSWER THEM.
YOU NEED US BOTH ALIVE UNTIL THE END.
IS THAT SO?
ONLY A FOOL WOULD ELIMINATE THE TWO PEOPLE WHO MADE ALL OF THIS POSSIBLE WITH INFORMATION THEY ALONE HAD.
PERHAPS I AM A FOOL THEN.
CARLOS. YOU MAY BEGIN.

THIS WILL BE AS EASY AS YOU MAKE IT.
PENETRATING THE FLESH ISN'T SO PAINFUL.
BUT WHEN HE TRIES TO PUSH THE NEEDLE THROUGH YOUR BONES, IT WILL BE.
WHAT ARE YOU THINKING?
LOFTIER THOUGHTS THAN YOU, I'M SURE.
PLEASE TRY TO CONTROL YOURSELF, MS. DE RAISON.
IT'S FINE, MONIQUE. DON'T BE AFRAID.
I'VE SEEN HOW THIS ENDS.
LET'S BEGIN WITH THIS KNOWLEDGE OF YOURS. HOW DID YOU FIND US?
I TALKED TO A LARGE WHITE BAT IN MY DREAMS. HE TOLD ME YOU WERE IN A MOUNTAIN CALLED CYCLOPS.
A BAT... OF COURSE.
CARLOS, PLEASE JOG MR. HUNTER'S MEMORY.

IT'S JUST A FEW CENTIMETERS IN NOW.
SO TELL ME THE FUTURE, THOMAS.
THERE ARE BOOKS IN MY DREAMS CALLED THE BOOKS OF HISTORIES. THEY'VE RECORDED EVERYTHING THAT'S HAPPENED HERE.
OVER HALF THE WORLD DIES FROM THE RAISON STRAIN.
THEN THE TIMES OF THE GREAT DECEPTION BEGINS.
OF COURSE, BUT I WAS REFERRING TO THE NEXT FEW DAYS. I WANT TO KNOW HOW WE WILL GET THERE.
I WANT TO KNOW WHAT THE AMERICANS WILL DO.
I DON'T KNOW.
CARLOS.
IT'S THE TRUTH.
I DON'T KNOW WHAT THE UNITED STATES WILL DO.
PERHAPS YOU SHOULD ASK THE WHITE BAT THEN.
CARLOS, ALL THE WAY TO THE BONE NOW, PLEASE.
UNNN
I WOULD HAVE EXPECTED MORE FROM HIM.
HE STILL HAS DRUGS IN HIS SYSTEM.
WE WILL HAVE TIME LATER. WE NEED TO MOVE BY NIGHTFALL.
CLEAN HIM UP. I WANT HIM LOOKING GOOD FOR FORTIER.

THUD!
THOMAS!
WHAT HAPPENED?
SORRY. I JUST...
WHAT'S THIS?
WHAT'S HAPPENING?
NOTHING.
IT'S JUST A SCRATCH.
THE NEEDLE.
WE NEED TO GO.
THEY'RE CALLING FOR YOU.
THE COUNCIL. JUSTIN IS COMING.
WHO IS?
HALF THE VILLAGE IS THERE TO RECEIVE HIM ALREADY.
TO RECEIVE HIM?

SO TELL ME. WHAT HAPPENED?
MY DREAMS, YOU MEAN.
WE FOUND MONIQUE.
I KNEW IT! IT'S ALL TRUE! I TOLD YOU TO BELIEVE ME THOMAS! SHE WAS THERE IN THE WHITE ROOM.
AS I RECALL IT WAS YOU WHO DIDN'T BELIEVE ME ONCE UPON A TIME.
THAT WAS THEN. SO YOU RESCUED ME?
NOT QUITE.
I'M WORKING ON IT.
NOT QUITE.
ISN'T IT POSSIBLE THAT ALL OF US LIVE IN BOTH WORLDS, THEN? IF YOU AND I DO.
I'VE THOUGHT ABOUT IT.
SO WHO IS QURONG THERE? AND WHO IS SVENSSON HERE?
IF WE FOUND SVENSSON HERE AND KILLED HIM, WOULDN'T HE DIE THERE?
I'M NOT SURE IT WORKS THAT WAY.
BESIDES, WE NEED SVENSSON ALIVE THERE. HE HAS THE ANTI-VIRUS.

THEN WHY AREN'T PEOPLE JUST FALLING OVER DEAD HERE WHEN THEY DIE THERE FROM AN ACCIDENT OR SOMETHING?
THEN MAYBE WE'RE ONLY PART OF THEM. THERE COULD BE OTHER REALITIES!
MAYBE THEY AREN'T CONNECTED UNLESS THEY KNOW.
THEN HOW DID I BREACH THESE REALITIES?
IT'S ONLY A THEORY.
I THINK I'M THE ONLY GATEWAY TO THESE REALITIES.
YET I WENT.
YOU WERE CUT WITH ME. AND BLEEDING. BOTH OF US WERE.
MAYBE THIS IS ALL NONSENSE.
IT MAY BE.
THOMAS! IT'S THOMAS OF HUNTER!

HUNTER!
HUNTER!
HUNTER!
HUNTER!
HUNTER!
HUNTER!
HUNTER!
HUNTER!
HUNTER!
HUNTER!
HUNTER!
HUNTER!
HUNTER!
JUSTIN!
JUSTIN!
JUSTIN!
JUSTIN!

ELYYOOOOON!
I SALUTE YOU, THOMAS OF HUNTER.

I TELL YOU ON THIS DAY, THAT THE GREATEST WARRIORS AMONG YOU ARE THE CHILDREN.
IT IS WITH ONES LIKE THESE THAT YOU WILL WAGE A NEW KIND OF WAR.
NOW DO YOU THINK THERE WILL BE A FIGHT AT THE CHALLENGE?
JUSTIN IS EITHER A MAN WHO DESERVES THIS PRAISE OR A MAN WHO DESERVES TO DIE.
WHO DO YOU THINK HE IS?
I THINK HE'S A DANGEROUS MAN.
BUT WE'LL LET THE PEOPLE DECIDE.

SEND THEM!
WE'RE RUNNING OUT OF TIME! WHAT CHOICE DO WE HAVE?
WE CAN REBUILD, START OVER, BUT WE NEED SOME BREATHING SPACE!
I *AM* THINKING OF SENDING THE MISSILES, DWIGHT. FULLY ARMED AND ON A COLLISION COURSE TO PARIS.
IF EITHER YOU OR ISRAEL DOES ANYTHING STUPID, YOU'LL SEND US ALL TO OUR GRAVES BASED ON THE ASSUMPTION THAT THEY ARE LYING TO US.
THEY'RE TERRORISTS, FOR CRYING OUT LOUD! HOW CAN WE TRUST THEM?
LOOK, THE SAME INTEL THAT'S TELLING US NOT TO TRUST THEM LOCATED SVENSSON.
YOU FOUND HIM?
YES, WE FOUND HIM. THEY SHOT DOWN OUR PLANE IN INDONESIA.
SO WE MAY FIND SVENSSON WITH THE ANTI-VIRUS?
YES.
HOW DID YOU FIND SVENSSON SO EASILY?
THOMAS HUNTER.

IN THIS ROOM.
WHAT WE SPEAK ABOUT IN HERE, STAYS IN HERE.
IF I LIKE WHAT I SEE, I MAY PLAY BALL.
BUT I'M NOT PROMISING ANYTHING.
YOU LEAK THIS AND I'LL HAVE YOU ARRESTED.
ON WHAT GROUNDS?
TREASON. LEAKING MILITARY OPERATIONS IS AN ACTIONABLE OFFENSE.
SIR, WE HAVE A REPORT FROM CYCLOPS!
THE SEARCH D RESCUE TEAM LOCATED THE WRECKAGE.
SURVIVORS?
NONE YET, SIR. BUT, THERE WAS SOMETHING ELSE. THE TACTICAL TEAM THAT WAS WITH THEM LOCATED AND ENTERED A LARGE COMPLEX THERE. IT WAS ABANDONED.
ABANDONED?
WITHIN THE LAST FEW HOURS. UT THERE'S EVIDENCE ONE OF OUR MEN WAS THERE.
HUNTER.
THEY CAN'T BE FAR.
FIND HIM!

THE GATHERING.
EVERY YEAR THE FOLLOWERS OF ELYON CAME TOGETHER. BUT THIS YEAR WAS DIFFERENT. THIS YEAR THE COUNCIL HAD ISSUED A CHALLENGE--
--TO LEARN THE TRUTH ABOUT JUSTIN'S TEACHINGS.
LOOK AT THEM, THOMAS. THERE ARE SOME HERE WHO THINK HE'S SOME KIND OF PROPHET.
JUSTIN'S JUST A MAN, MIKIL.
YES, AND WHEN THE COUNCIL RULES AGAINST HIM, THEY'LL WANT YOU TO FIGHT HIM.
EVEN IF THERE IS A FIGHT, I WON'T KILL HIM.
HE'S POISONING THE MINDS OF OUR PEOPLE. SOMEONE HAS TO PUT A STOP TO IT.
AND WE WILL, BUT A MAN'S IDEAS SHOULDN'T SENTENCE HIM TO DEATH. BANISHMENT IS ENOUGH.
BESIDES, I DON'T HAVE TIME FOR THIS. I HAVE TO GO AFTER THE BOOKS OF HISTORIES...
THEY'RE COMING!

THE COUNCIL.
WHERE'S JUSTIN?
THE COUNCIL WILL ISSUE ITS CHALLENGE OF THE PHILOSOPHIES OF JUSTIN OF SOUTHERN IN THIS TENTH ANNUAL GATHERING OF ALL FOREST PEOPLE.
JUSTIN, WE CALL YOU FORTH.
HE'S GOING TO DEFAULT.
HE KNOWS THAT HE'S WRONG.
WAIT— WHO'S THAT?
THAT'S HIM.
JUSTIN OF SOUTHERN ACCEPTS YOUR CHALLENGE.

THE MAN WE SEE HERE IS A MIGHTY WARRIOR A MAN WHO LOVES CHILDREN AND ACCEPTS PRAISE WITH GRACIOUSNESS.
FOR EACH OF THESE WE HONOR JUSTIN OF SOUTHERN.
NEVERTHELESS, IT IS SAID HE SPREADS POISONOUS BLASPHEMY AGAINST ELYON THROUGH THE SOUTHERN FOREST.
WE ARE ASSEMBLED TO LEARN THE TRUTH OF THIS CLAIM.
WE JUDGE NOT THE MAN, ONLY HIS DOCTRINE.
IS IT NOT TRUE THAT THE HORDE IS THE ENEMY OF ELYON?
IT IS TRUE.
AND IS IT NOT TRUE THAT THOSE WHO CONSPIRE WITH ELYON'S ENEMIES CONSPIRE AGAINST ELYON HIMSELF?
IT IS TRUE.
AND IS IT TRUE THAT YOU ADVOCATE NEGOTIATING A PEACE WITH THE HORDE?
IT IS TRUE.
YOU *DO* KNOW SUCH A THING IS TREASON. YET YOU WISH TO MAKE PEACE WITH THEM? IT IS BLASPHEMOUS.

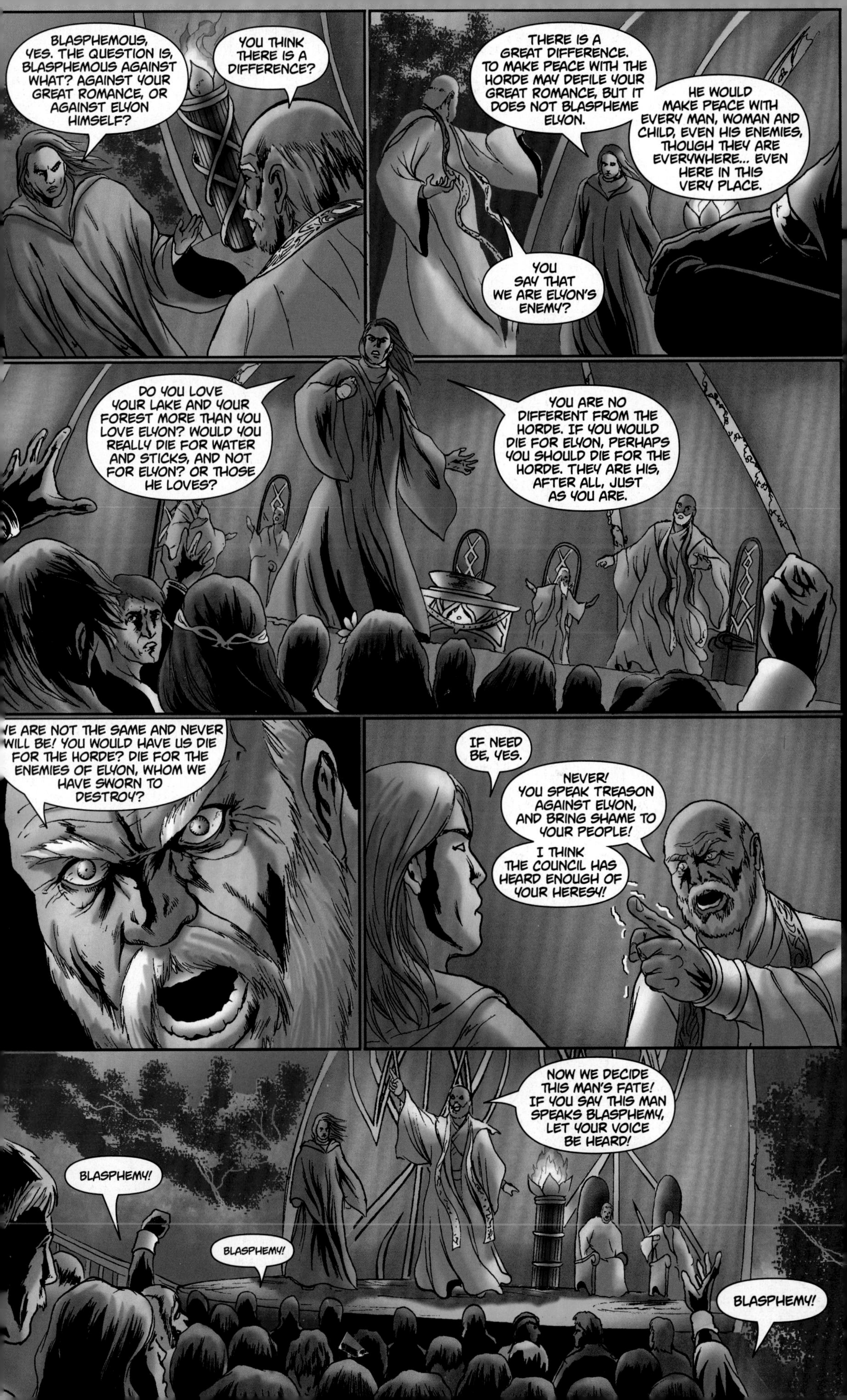
BLASPHEMOUS, YES. THE QUESTION IS, BLASPHEMOUS AGAINST WHAT? AGAINST YOUR GREAT ROMANCE, OR AGAINST ELYON HIMSELF?
YOU THINK THERE IS A DIFFERENCE?
THERE IS A GREAT DIFFERENCE. TO MAKE PEACE WITH THE HORDE MAY DEFILE YOUR GREAT ROMANCE, BUT IT DOES NOT BLASPHEME ELYON.
HE WOULD MAKE PEACE WITH EVERY MAN, WOMAN AND CHILD, EVEN HIS ENEMIES, THOUGH THEY ARE EVERYWHERE... EVEN HERE IN THIS VERY PLACE.
YOU SAY THAT WE ARE ELYON'S ENEMY?
DO YOU LOVE YOUR LAKE AND YOUR FOREST MORE THAN YOU LOVE ELYON? WOULD YOU REALLY DIE FOR WATER AND STICKS, AND NOT FOR ELYON? OR THOSE HE LOVES?
YOU ARE NO DIFFERENT FROM THE HORDE. IF YOU WOULD DIE FOR ELYON, PERHAPS YOU SHOULD DIE FOR THE HORDE. THEY ARE HIS, AFTER ALL, JUST AS YOU ARE.
WE ARE NOT THE SAME AND NEVER WILL BE! YOU WOULD HAVE US DIE FOR THE HORDE? DIE FOR THE ENEMIES OF ELYON, WHOM WE HAVE SWORN TO DESTROY?
IF NEED BE, YES.
NEVER! YOU SPEAK TREASON AGAINST ELYON, AND BRING SHAME TO YOUR PEOPLE!
I THINK THE COUNCIL HAS HEARD ENOUGH OF YOUR HERESY!
NOW WE DECIDE THIS MAN'S FATE! IF YOU SAY THIS MAN SPEAKS BLASPHEMY, LET YOUR VOICE BE HEARD!
BLASPHEMY!
BLASPHEMY!
BLASPHEMY!

I CALL OUR DEFENDER, THOMAS OF HUNTER!
I CALL HIM TO DEFEND OUR TRUTH AGAINST THIS BLASPHEMY... IN A FIGHT TO THE DEATH!
I WILL, BUT I SEEK BANISHMENT, NOT DEATH.
YOU HAVE NO CHOICE.
FIGHT! FIGHT TO TH DEATH!
YOU'RE A GOOD MAN, THOMAS.
I ALWAYS LIKED YOU. AND I STILL DO, VERY MUCH.
I DON'T WANT TO KILL, BUT I WILL IF I HAVE TO.
YOU MEAN, IF YOU CAN.
KRANNNG
KLANK
YOU HAVE NO IDEA WHAT YOU'VE GOTTEN YOURSELF INTO. BE CAREFUL.
ARE YOU GOING TO TALK...

...OR FIGHT?!
YOU'RE A BETTER WARRIOR THAN THE OTHERS.
AM I?
THEN LET ME FIGHT YOU WITHOUT A SWORD. LET ME SHOW YOU HOW THIS WAR WILL BE WON.
THE ONLY WAY IT CAN BE WON IS WITH BLOOD.
YOU DECEIVE THE PEOPLE INTO BELIEVING THERE CAN BE PEACE.
AND AT THIS VERY MOMENT THE HORDE IS PLANNING A BETRAYAL.
THUD!
KILL HIM!
NOW! KILL HIM!
HE WANTS ME TO KILL YOU.
I CAN. BUT I WON'T.
WHACK

YOU SHOULD HAVE WATCHED YOUR FOOTING, THOMAS.
SEE HOW QUICKLY THE TABLES CAN TURN?
ENOUGH FIGHTING. NOW I WILL SHOW YOU THE WAY TO PEACE.
COME FORWARD MARTYN.
MARTYN? IMPOSSIBLE! I KILLED HIM IN QURONG'S TENT!
I BRING YOU THE MAN WITH WHOM I WILL NEGOTIATE A PEACE BETWEEN THE DESERT DWELLERS AND FOREST PEOPLE.
I GAVE HIM MY WORD THAT YOU WOULD NOT KILL HIM. HIS ARMIES ARE CLOSE NOW AND COULD SWARM THE FOREST AND DESTROY ALL OF YOU.
BUT IF ELYON'S CHILDREN WERE TO DIE, WHO WOULD BE VICTOR?
AAAAII!
NO! THOMAS! YOU DO NOT KNOW WHO THIS MAN IS!
YOU KNOW THIS MAN WELL. BUT, BY ANOTHER NAME.
YOU KNEW HIM ONCE AS JOHAN.
BROTHER?
CAN IT BE?

SOMEWHERE IN THE FRENCH COUNTRYSIDE.
COME NOW, THE DRUGS MUST BE WEARING OFF BY NOW.
JUST SO YOU KNOW, THOMAS, THE AMERICANS DID TRY AND RESCUE YOU.
THEY WANT YOU, THOMAS.
EVERYONE SEEMS TO WANT THOMAS HUNTER. AS IF YOU'RE THE MESSIAH OR SOMETHING.
I KNOW WHO YOU ARE.
IS THAT SO? PERHAPS YOU KNOW SOME OTHER THINGS AS WELL.
SUCH AS, HOW FAR WILL THE PRESIDENT CARRY HIS BLUFF?
WE ARE FULLY PREPARED FOR A NUCLEAR EXCHANGE. KNOWING IF AND WHEN THEY MIGHT ATTACK WOULD BE...HELPFUL.
HE WON'T FIRE THEM.
NO? MAYBE YOU DON'T KNOW THE PRESIDENT LIKE I DO.
WE ARE GOING PUBLIC IN FRANCE IN THREE DAYS.
OVER A HUNDRED OF THE... LESS-PROGRESSIVE MEMBERS OF THE GOVERNMENT WILL MEET UNTIMELY ENDS BETWEEN NOW AND THEN.
SO AS YOU CAN SEE, I'M A BUSY MAN.
WE'LL TALK AGAIN SOON... LET'S HOPE FOR YOUR SAKE YOUR MEMORY SERVES YOU BETTER.

LET'S GO. I'M MOVING YOU TO ANOTHER ROOM. DON'T MAKE ME DRAG YOU.
NOW. I WON'T ASK AGAIN.
CARLOS, WE NEED TO TALK.
I WOULD RATHER SLICE YOUR TONGUE OUT THAN LISTEN TO YOUR TALK.
IT'S ABOUT THE FRENCHMAN.
IT HAS TO DO WITH HOW I KNEW WHERE TO FIND MONIQUE.
WHAT DOES THIS HAVE TO DO WITH FORTIER?
YOU KNOW ABOUT MY DREAMS, DON'T YOU?
THIS IS A POINTLESS DISCUSSION.
ALL OF IT'S TRUE. I CAN PASS BETWEEN TWO REALITIES THROUGH MY DREAMS. THAT'S HOW I KNEW ABOUT THE VIRUS, WHERE MONIQUE WAS... EVERYTHING.
THAT WORLD IS AS REAL AS THIS ONE, CARLOS.
AND I THINK YOU ARE CONNECTED TO THIS OTHER WORLD AS WELL.
IMPOSSIBLE.
YOU DON'T HAVE A MEMORY OF IT YET, BUT YOU WILL SOON.
THERE YOUR NAME IS JOHAN AND YOU ARE THE BROTHER OF MY WIFE.
DON'T BE RIDICULOUS! STOP THIS AT ONCE!
WHAT IF I COULD PROVE IT TO YOU, BROTHER?

THEN I'LL PROVE IT. I CUT JOHAN ON THE NECK AND I THINK IT MAY HAVE TRANSLATED INTO THIS WORLD.
STOP THIS NONSENSE!
LET MY ACTIONS SPEAK THE TRUTH. TOUCH YOUR NECK.
YOU LIVE IN THE OTHER REALITY TOO, BUT AS JOHAN. WE HAD A CONFRONTATION AT THE GATHERING.
I CUT YOUR NECK WITH MY SWORD.
DO YOU BELIEVE, CARLOS?
HOW CAN THIS BE?
THIS IS WITCHCRAFT.
OF COURSE YOU DO. YOU'VE ALWAYS BELIEVED, HAVEN'T YOU?
NO, NOT WITCHCRAFT. REALITY. THE SKIN BETWEEN TWO WORLDS PEELING BACK.
BUT HOW?
HUUUNH
WHACK!
QUICK! THE KEYS ARE IN HIS RIGHT POCKET.

C'MON. GIVE ME YOUR HAND.
WE GO STRAIGHT FOR THE FOREST.
ONCE WE RUN, WE DON'T STOP. WE DON'T LOOK BACK.
NO MATTER WHAT HAPPENS, OK?
OK.
IF WE GET SEPARATED, FIND A CAR. GET HELP. WE HAVE TO GET TO THE PRESIDENT.
GO!
I KNEW YOU WOULD TRY TO RUN.
SO I TOOK THE LIBERTY OF POSTING SOME... INSURANCE.
AAAAHH!
CRACK!
THOMAS!
RUN!
CRACK!
RUN! DON'T LOOK BACK.

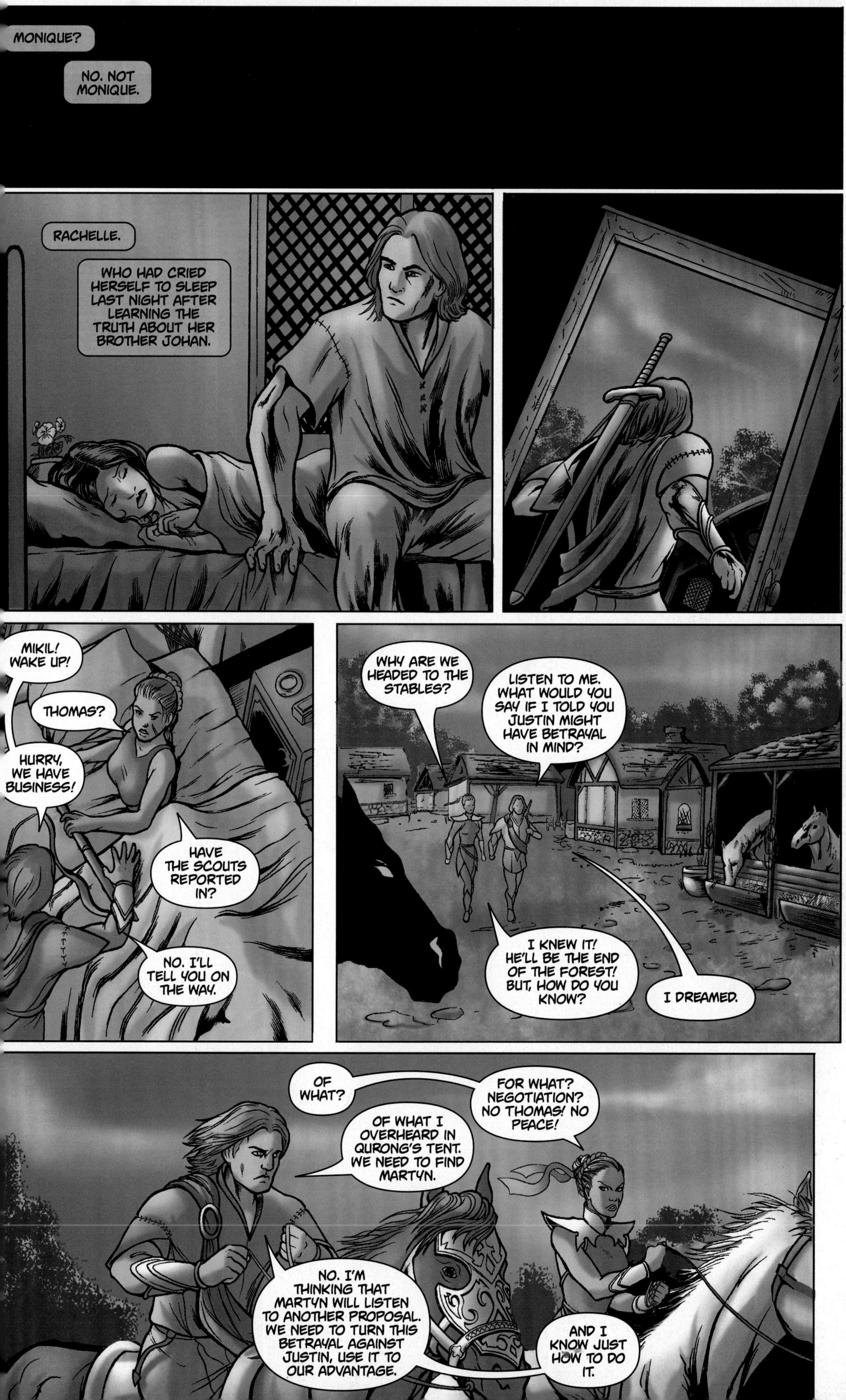
MONIQUE?
NO. NOT MONIQUE.
RACHELLE.
WHO HAD CRIED HERSELF TO SLEEP LAST NIGHT AFTER LEARNING THE TRUTH ABOUT HER BROTHER JOHAN.
MIKIL! WAKE UP!
THOMAS?
HURRY, WE HAVE BUSINESS!
HAVE THE SCOUTS REPORTED IN?
NO. I'LL TELL YOU ON THE WAY.
WHY ARE WE HEADED TO THE STABLES?
LISTEN TO ME. WHAT WOULD YOU SAY IF I TOLD YOU JUSTIN MIGHT HAVE BETRAYAL IN MIND?
I KNEW IT! HE'LL BE THE END OF THE FOREST! BUT, HOW DO YOU KNOW?
I DREAMED.
OF WHAT?
OF WHAT I OVERHEARD IN QURONG'S TENT. WE NEED TO FIND MARTYN.
FOR WHAT? NEGOTIATION? NO THOMAS! NO PEACE!
NO. I'M THINKING THAT MARTYN WILL LISTEN TO ANOTHER PROPOSAL. WE NEED TO TURN THIS BETRAYAL AGAINST JUSTIN, USE IT TO OUR ADVANTAGE.
AND I KNOW JUST HOW TO DO IT.

RUN!
DON'T LOOK BACK.
THOMAS?
THE HANDCUFFS.
MORNING MOTHER.
MARIE, WHERE IS YOUR FATHER?
I DON'T KNOW. HE LEFT EARLY. BEFORE THE SUN WAS UP. I HEARD HIM.
HE WENT AFTER JUSTIN.
JUSTIN WAS WITH MARTYN.
WITH THE HORDE.
I HAVE TO FIND HIM. IF HE WAS HURT IN MY DREAM, DOES THAT MEAN...
WHERE DID THEY COME FROM?
A GUARD PATROL.
ELYON, HELP ME...

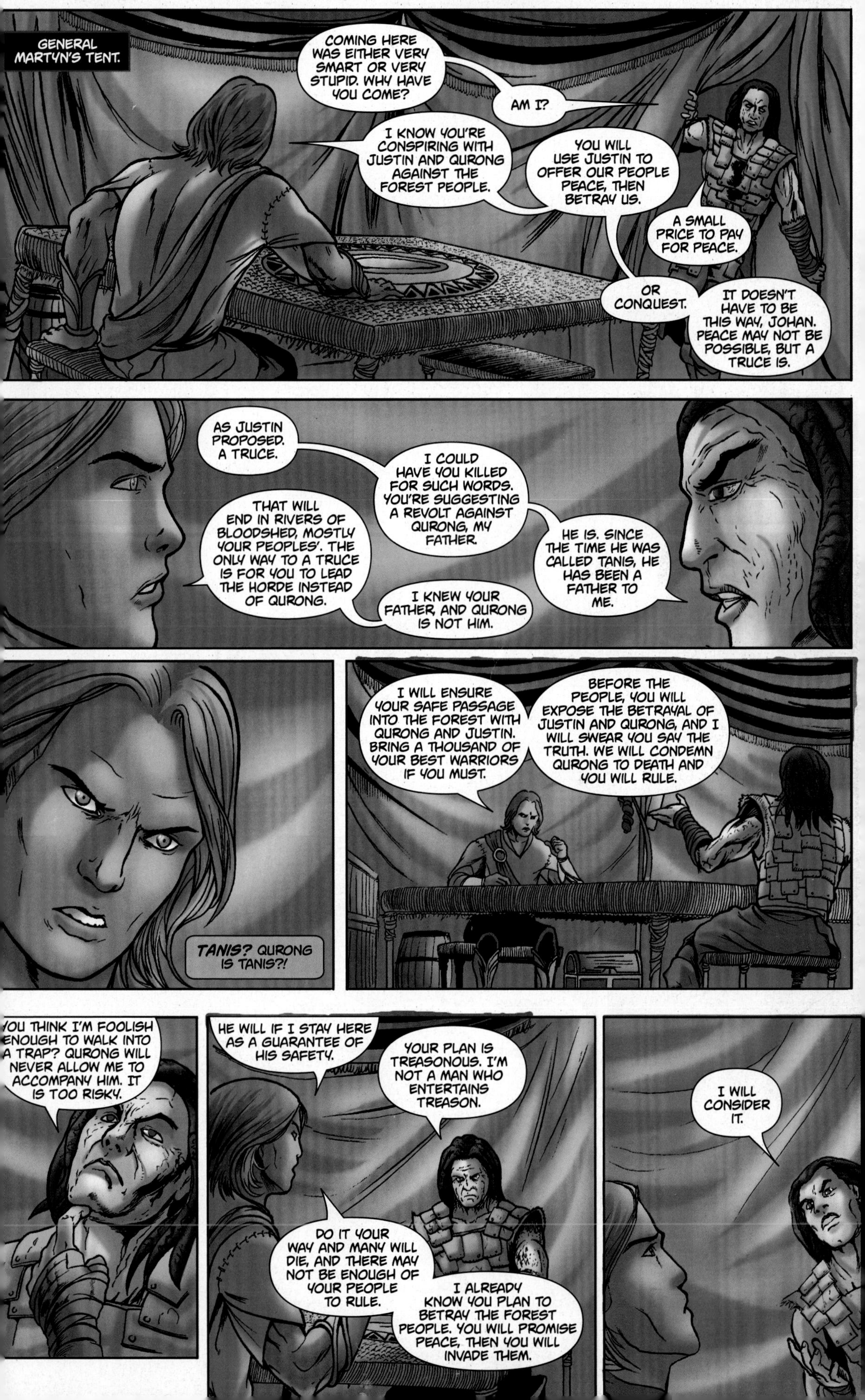
GENERAL MARTYN'S TENT.
COMING HERE WAS EITHER VERY SMART OR VERY STUPID. WHY HAVE YOU COME?
AM I?
I KNOW YOU'RE CONSPIRING WITH JUSTIN AND QURONG AGAINST THE FOREST PEOPLE.
YOU WILL USE JUSTIN TO OFFER OUR PEOPLE PEACE, THEN BETRAY US.
A SMALL PRICE TO PAY FOR PEACE.
OR CONQUEST.
IT DOESN'T HAVE TO BE THIS WAY, JOHAN. PEACE MAY NOT BE POSSIBLE, BUT A TRUCE IS.
AS JUSTIN PROPOSED. A TRUCE.
I COULD HAVE YOU KILLED FOR SUCH WORDS. YOU'RE SUGGESTING A REVOLT AGAINST QURONG, MY FATHER.
THAT WILL END IN RIVERS OF BLOODSHED, MOSTLY YOUR PEOPLES'. THE ONLY WAY TO A TRUCE IS FOR YOU TO LEAD THE HORDE INSTEAD OF QURONG.
HE IS. SINCE THE TIME HE WAS CALLED TANIS, HE HAS BEEN A FATHER TO ME.
I KNEW YOUR FATHER, AND QURONG IS NOT HIM.
TANIS? QURONG IS TANIS?!
I WILL ENSURE YOUR SAFE PASSAGE INTO THE FOREST WITH QURONG AND JUSTIN. BRING A THOUSAND OF YOUR BEST WARRIORS IF YOU MUST.
BEFORE THE PEOPLE, YOU WILL EXPOSE THE BETRAYAL OF JUSTIN AND QURONG, AND I WILL SWEAR YOU SAY THE TRUTH. WE WILL CONDEMN QURONG TO DEATH AND YOU WILL RULE.
YOU THINK I'M FOOLISH ENOUGH TO WALK INTO A TRAP? QURONG WILL NEVER ALLOW ME TO ACCOMPANY HIM. IT IS TOO RISKY.
HE WILL IF I STAY HERE AS A GUARANTEE OF HIS SAFETY.
YOUR PLAN IS TREASONOUS. I'M NOT A MAN WHO ENTERTAINS TREASON.
DO IT YOUR WAY AND MANY WILL DIE, AND THERE MAY NOT BE ENOUGH OF YOUR PEOPLE TO RULE.
I ALREADY KNOW YOU PLAN TO BETRAY THE FOREST PEOPLE. YOU WILL PROMISE PEACE, THEN YOU WILL INVADE THEM.
I WILL CONSIDER IT.

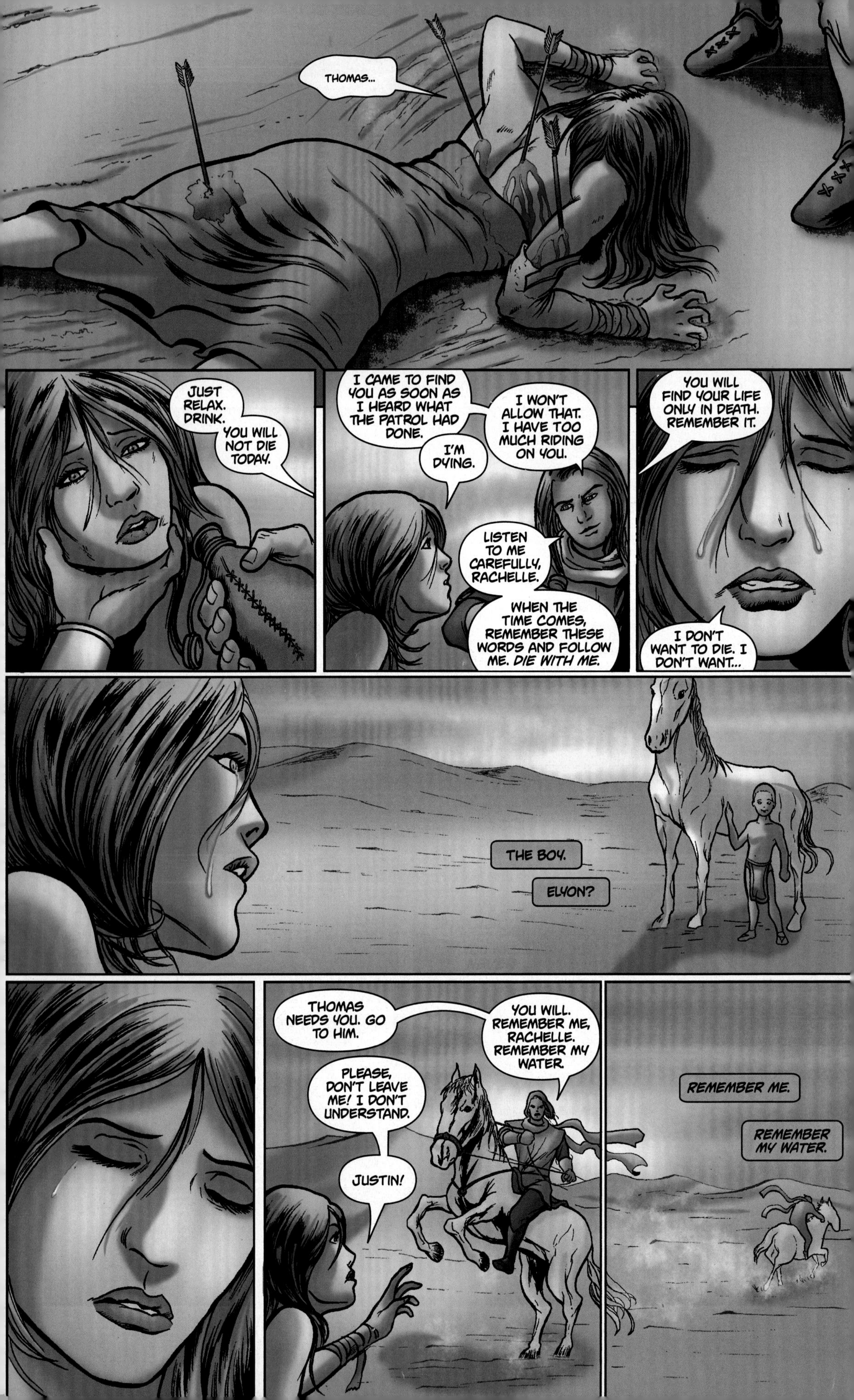

THOMAS...
JUST RELAX. DRINK.
YOU WILL NOT DIE TODAY.
I CAME TO FIND YOU AS SOON AS I HEARD WHAT THE PATROL HAD DONE.
I WON'T ALLOW THAT. I HAVE TOO MUCH RIDING ON YOU.
I'M DYING.
LISTEN TO ME CAREFULLY, RACHELLE.
WHEN THE TIME COMES, REMEMBER THESE WORDS AND FOLLOW ME. *DIE WITH ME.*
YOU WILL FIND YOUR LIFE ONLY IN DEATH. REMEMBER IT.
I DON'T WANT TO DIE. I DON'T WANT...
THE BOY.
ELYON?
THOMAS NEEDS YOU. GO TO HIM.
YOU WILL. REMEMBER ME, RACHELLE. REMEMBER MY WATER.
PLEASE, DON'T LEAVE ME! I DON'T UNDERSTAND.
JUSTIN!
REMEMBER ME.
REMEMBER MY WATER.

MEANWHILE...
I DON'T LIKE IT, THOMAS.
YOU'RE JUST GOING TO LET THEM TAKE YOU IN SHACKLES?
NOT "JUST", MIKIL. AS LONG AS YOU HAVE QURONG AND MARTYN, I'M SAFE.
JUSTIN HAS BROKERED PEACE AND YOU'RE IN AGREEMENT.
JUSTIN IS BROKERING PEACE. FOR THE MOMENT I AM IN AGREEMENT.
THE COUNCIL WILL NEVER ACCEPT.
THEY WILL. JUST DO AS I TOLD YOU.
IT'S COME DOWN TO THIS AFTER ALL, MY BROTHER.
THAT'S WHAT YOU WANTED, ISN'T IT? PEACE?
I KNEW YOU'D COME.
IF YOU KNOW SO MUCH, THEN DO YOU KNOW IF I'LL BE SAFE IN THEIR SHACKLES?
I THINK YOU'LL BE SAFER IN THEIR HANDS THAN I WILL BE WITH OUR OWN COUNCIL.
TAKE COURAGE, THOMAS. I'LL SEE YOU IN THE LAKE. SOON.

THOMAS!
WUHRACK!
DON'T LOOK BACK.
FIND HELP.
RUN! I HAVE A LOT RIDING ON YOU.

THOMAS!
I NEED TO SEE THOMAS OF HUNTER!
WHAT BUSINESS DO YOU HAVE?
I AM HERE BECAUSE MY LORD NEEDS ME!
JUSTIN OF SOUTHERN SENT YOU?
THAT'S RIGHT. JUSTIN OF SOUTHERN SENT ME. I AM TO RETURN WITH WORD OF HUNTER'S HEALTH.
FOLLOW ME.

THOMAS!
WE DID NOTHING TO HIM.
YOU SHOULD KNOW THIS– HIS WOUNDS ARE SELF-INFLICTED.
THOMAS...
OUT! GET OUT!
LEAVE!
THOMAS...

THOMAS... PLEASE.
ELYON, PLEASE. PLEASE, SAVE HIM.
THOMAS!
REMEMBER ME. REMEMBER MY WATER.
ELYON'S WATER.
PLEASE... THOMAS... PLEASE.

≥GAAASP≤
RACHELLE?
BE QUIET—THEY'RE OUTSIDE.
WE'RE IN THE HORDE CAMP.
YOU WERE DEAD... ELYON'S WATER HEALED YOU.
HIS WATER HEALS AGAIN?
YES. HE HEALED ME TOO.
IT'S HIM, THOMAS.
WHO?
JUSTIN. JUSTIN IS THE BOY. HE'S THE BOY.
WHAT?
DON'T YOU SEE? THE SIGNS WERE ALL THERE, WE JUST DIDN'T SEE THEM. OR DIDN'T WANT TO SEE THEM.
THE PROPHECY...
ONE DAY, WHEN YOU THINK IT CAN'T GET ANY WORSE, THERE WILL BE A WAY.
IN ONE INCREDIBLE BLOW WE WILL DESTROY THE HEART OF EVIL.
MY DEAR, DEAR GOD, ELYON!
WHAT?
I'VE BETRAYED HIM. IT'S A SETUP. ALL OF IT.
WE'VE GOT TO GET OUT OF HERE.
THEY'RE GOING TO KILL HIM.

I HAVE PUT MY LIFE IN YOUR HANDS TO MEET YOU. SURELY YOU WILL CONSIDER MY PROPOSAL FOR A TRUCE, AT LONG LAST.
FOR THE SAKE OF PEACE, WE ARE ALWAYS WILLING TO LISTEN.
BUT WE SEE NO BASIS FOR PEACE. YOU LIVE IN VIOLATION OF ELYON'S LAWS. FOR THAT YOU DESERVE DEATH, NOT PEACE.
AND HOW MANY OF US MUST YOU KILL TO SATISFY YOUR GOD?
WE HAVE NO BASIS FOR TRUST BETWEEN OUR PEOPLE AND YOURS BECAUSE YOU SEE US AS DOGS.
YOU LIVE IN DEATH ALREADY!
YOU'RE RIGHT! WE DON'T TRUST YOU. WE HAVE NO REASON TO.
THEN I WILL OFFER YOU MORE THAN THE WORDS OF A DOG TODAY, AS A SHOW OF GOOD FAITH AND OUR DESIRE FOR PEACE.
WE CAME TODAY WITH BETRAYAL ON OUR MINDS. WE HAD PLANNED TO OFFER PEACE, THEN CRUSH YOU WITH OUR ARMY, WHICH IS ALREADY CAMPED AROUND YOU.
BUT I SEE THAT A PEACE ACCORD IS THE ONLY WAY. I WILL DISPATCH RIDERS WITH WORD FOR MY GENERAL'S TO PULL BACK TO THE DESERT.
IN THE INTEREST OF PEACE.
THEN WHAT DO YOU PROPOSE? THAT WE OFFER YOU PEACE BECAUSE YOU CONFESSED YOUR INTENT TO RUIN US?

I PROPOSE TO MEET THE REQUIREMENT OF YOUR LAWS.
HOW? BY CONFESSING? IT'S NOT ENOUGH.
NO. BY GIVING YOU THE MAN WHO WOULD BETRAY YOU AND LEAD US TO WAR. YOU MUST KNOW, THIS BETRAYAL WAS NOT MY IDEA.
THEN WHOSE WAS IT?
IT WAS HIS.
IT WAS JUSTIN WHO CLAIMED OUR VICTORY WOULD BE COMPLETE BY OFFERING PEACE!
HOW DARE YOU ACCUSE ONE OF OUR OWN TO SAVE YOURSELF!
IT IS TRUE! I CAN CORROBORATE!
AND I CAN DO SO WITH THOMAS OF HUNTER'S AUTHORITY!
HE IS IN THE HORDE CAMP NOW, GUARANTEEING QURONG'S SAFETY SO WE CAN EXPOSE THE TRUTH OF JUSTIN'S BETRAYAL--
YOUR LAWS REQUIRE DEATH FOR DEFILEMENT OF ELYON'S LOVE. WHAT GREATER DEFILEMENT IS THERE THAN BETRAYAL?
THERE IS NONE.
HE HAS ALSO WAGED WAR AGAINST OUR PEOPLE. FOR THAT, OUR LAW ALSO REQUIRES HIS DEATH. HIS DEATH WILL SATISFY BOTH OF OUR LAWS...AND SEAL OUR PEACE.

STEP OUT, JUSTIN.
WHAT SAY YOU TO THESE CHARGES? IS THIS TRUE?
I HAVE FULFILLED YOUR LAWS, BATHED IN THE LAKES, AND LOVED ALL THAT ELYON LOVES.
HAVE YOU CONSPIRED TO BETRAY ELYON'S PEOPLE?
ANSWER ME!
HAVE YOU BECOME SO BLIND, CIPHUS, THAT YOU CANNOT REMEMBER ME?
WHAT?
HAS IT BEEN SO LONG SINCE WE SWAM TOGETHER?
YOUR DECEITFUL WORDS WILL NOT CONVINCE ME TRAITOR!
I AM AN ELDER OF ELYON'S COUNCIL.
THEN YOU SHOULD KNOW THE ANSWER TO YOUR QUESTION, CIPHUS.
ANSWER ME OR I'LL CONDEMN YOU MYSELF!
WHAT SAY YOU?

VERY WELL. THEN FOR THE TREASON AGAINST ELYON AND HIS PEOPLE, YOU WILL DIE AT THE HANDS OF YOUR ENEMIES. YOU WILL DIE A HORDE DEATH.
LET JUSTICE BEEN DONE, AND MAY OUR PEACE BE SEALED WITH HIS BLOOD.
ONE LIFE FOR THE MANY.
INTERESTING, ISN'T IT, HOW EASILY YOUR PEOPLE CAN KILL WHEN IT'S IN ELYON'S NAME?
I'M GOING TO TAKE GREAT PLEASURE IN YOUR SUFFERING.
SOON YOU WILL BEG FOR DEATH.
I ONLY REGRET THAT I CAN KILL YOU ONLY ONCE.
STRIP HIM AND TIE HIM!
TODAY WE DELIVER JUSTICE TO THIS MAN!

FOR OVER AN HOUR THE DULL SOUND OF THICK METAL RODS LANDING ON JUSTIN FILLED THE AIR.
HE NEVER CRIED OUT, EVEN WHEN THE SOUND OF SPLINTERING BONE COULD BE HEARD DEEP WITHIN THE CROWD.
STOP! STOP!
STOP THIS!
WHAT IS THIS? WHO AUTHORIZED THIS?
TWACK!
STAND DOWN THOMAS UNLESS YOU WISH TO JOIN HIM.
NO! NO!
STOP! YOU DON'T UNDERSTAND!
WE HAVE TO STOP THIS!
WE WILL NOT! THAT WOULD DEFY THE ORDER OF COUNCIL AND ELYON HIMSELF!
THE VERDICT HAS BEEN CAST. THE FATE OF OUR PEOPLE DEPENDS ON THIS EXCHANGE.
ARE YOU SO BLIND? THE PEACE WON'T LAST! YOU THINK YOU CAN TRUST THESE SCABS TO KEEP PEACE? IT'S ALL A LIE!
QURONG IS TANIS! HE'S BLINDED BY TEELEH, AND HE'S FOUND A WAY TO KILL ELYON!
ELYON WOULD NEVER LET A SCAB ABUSE HIM, ANY MORE THAN HE WOULD LET TEELEH ABUSE HIM.
IF HE IS ELYON, THEN LET HIM SAVE HIMSELF. HE IS A MAN, THOMAS. A MAN.
THE TIME HAS COME.
TO THE TOWER.

SET THE TOWER IN THE LAKE...
AND PREPARE HIM FOR THE DROWNING.
A HORDE DROWNING.
IT WOULD BE A SLOW DEATH.
LIFT HIM UP!

JOHAN?
REMEMBER...
REMEMBER ME.
REMEMBER ME JOHAN!
DROWN HIM!
HE'S NOT HOLDING HIS BREATH.
HE'S TRYING TO BREATHE THE WATER IN.
SPLOOSH!
IT WENT ON FOR WHAT SEEMED AN ETERNITY, UNTIL...
THOMAS... HIS SKIN. HE HAS THE DISEASE.
ELYON...
JOHAN, WHAT ARE YOU DOING?
BRINGING PEACE, THOMAS. OR HAVE YOU FORGOTTEN ALREADY?
IT'S TIME TO END THIS.

TELL ME JUSTIN, IS THIS THE BEST ELYON CAN DO?
PATHETIC.
AAARGAHH!
SSLIIKKK!
CUT HIM DOWN.
IT IS FINISHED.

JUSTIN'S DEATH SEALED THE PEACE BETWEEN THE DESERT DWELLERS AND THE FOREST PEOPLE. THE TREATY WAS SIGNED AND THE HORDE LEFT THE FOREST.
NOTHING WOULD EVER BE THE SAME AGAIN.
NOTHING.
THE FOLLOWING MORNING.
WHAT'S THIS?
OUR SKIN. IT'S BEGINNING TO CHANGE.
IT'S THE DISEASE. BUT, HOW?
IN ONE NIGHT?
WHAT'S HAPPENING?
I DON'T KNOW, BUT WE SHOULD GET TO THE LAKE AND BATHE.
FATHER, MY SKIN HURTS.
MINE TOO.

NO.
THOMAS, WHAT'S HAPPENING?
I...I DON'T KNOW.
THE POWER...
...IT'S GONE.
WE'RE BECOMING LIKE THEM...
WE'RE BECOMING LIKE THE HORDE!
THOMAS, THE HORDE IS COMING. WHAT DO WE DO?
WHAT DOYOU MEAN THEY'RE COMING?
SUZAN JUST SENT WORD. BOTH ARMIES ARE IN THE FOREST. THEY ARE AT OUR DOORSTEP!
BOTH? HOW MANY? HOW FAR?
TOO MANY. IT DOESN'T MATTER. MY MEN ARE ALL DISEASED.
ELYON IS PUNISHING US. LOOK AT THE LAKE! HE WAS INNOCENT!
JOHAN KNEW. HE KNEW JUSTIN WAS PURE AND HE KNEW THAT INNOCENT BLOOD WOULD POISON ELYON'S LAKE.
I KNOW WHAT WE MUST DO.
JUSTIN TOLD ME TO DIE WITH HIM. DROWN WITH HIM, THOMAS LIKE WE DID YEARS AGO.
THOMAS, YOU HAVE TO LISTEN TO ME!
YOU'RE SUGGESTING WE RUN INTO THIS LAKE AND DROWN OURSELVES? KILL OURSELVES?!
YOU WOULD RATHER LIVE LIKE THIS?

FOLLOW ME, THOMAS.
SWIM WITH ME.
DIE WITH ME.
I REMEMBER, RACHELLE. I REMEMBER NOW.
HE...SPOKE TO ME IN MY SLEEP.
ELYON. HE SPOKE TO ME.
I KNEW HE WAS INNOCENT.
IT WAS MY IDEA. I PLANNED ALL OF THIS WITH QURONG. TO DESTROY THE LAKES. TO UNITE OUR PEOPLE...
I EVEN KNEW WHO HE WAS!
AND NOW I'VE MURDERED HIM.
WHAT HAVE I DONE?
LOOK!
SHATAIKI. THEY HAVEN'T BEEN SEEN IN YEARS.
RACHELLE, JOHAN...DIVE INTO THE LAKE. WE HAVE TO DROWN!
ELYON IS ASKING US TO DROWN.
DIE WITH ME.
BUT HOW?
DIVE DEEP, AS DEEP AS YOU CAN GO, AND DIE WITH ME.

DIVE DEEP, THOMAS.
IN DYING, YOU WILL FIND LIFE. ALL OF YOU.
I BEG YOU! TAKE ME! YOU MADE ME, NOW TAKE ME.
OPEN YOUR MOUTH, THOMAS. BREATHE IT IN.
REMEMBER ME, THOMAS.
YOU'LL FIND LIFE IN DEATH.
GAASSP
RACHELLE. JOHAN? THE DISEASE IS GONE.
IT WAS ELYON. THOMAS... WE FOLLOWED.
WE DROWNED, JUST AS YOU DID.
QUICK, WE MUST TELL THE OTHERS!

ALL OF YOU WHO WILL FOLLOW JUSTIN IN HIS DEATH AND FIND NEW LIFE, LISTEN TO ME!
SWIM AS DEEP AS YOU CAN AND DROWN. DIE.
YOU WOULD HAVE US KILL OURSELVES?
YES! COME AND DIE. COME!
SEVENTEEN FOLLOWED AND DOVE INTO THE LAKE. THEY DROWNED, AND FOUND LIFE. BUT, MOST DID NOT FOLLOW.
THERE ISN'T MUCH TIME. THEIR FORCES WILL BE HERE SOON. READY THE HORSES.
WE RIDE THROUGH THE FOREST?
YES. NORTH. I'LL BRING EVERY-ONE TO THE STABLES.
LET'S HOPE THERE IS ENOUGH TIME.
JOHAN WILL TAKE THE CHILDREN BY WAY OF THE MEADOW.
WE'LL DRAW THE HORDE AWAY UNTIL THEY'RE CLEAR...
...THEN MEET AT THE APPLE GROVE BEYOND THE RIDGE.
HANG ON!
MMMNN
RACHELLE! HANG ON! RACHELLE!
SHE'S HIT THOMAS! RACHELLE'S BEEN HIT!
DIVERT THEM WILLIAM! I HAVE TO GET HER OUT OF HERE!

MIKIL! I NEED YOU!
MAMA? MAMA!
MIKIL, PLEASE HELP HER.
THEY ARE TOO DEEP. IT'S TOO MUCH BLOOD.
THOMAS, I'M SORRY.
THERE'S NOTHING WE CAN DO FOR HER.
MOUNT. LEAD THEM TO THE GROVE. WAIT FOR US THERE.
THOMAS? THOMAS, WE NEED TO MOVE. THEY'LL BE HERE SOON.
GIVE HER BACK.
WHAT?
GIVE HER BACK!
MY DAUGHTER IS WITH ME NOW, THOMAS. I NEED HER.
RIDE WITH ME. MEET ME AT THE DESERT.
BUT, I NEED HER MORE THAN YOU DO!
RIDE WITH ME. TRUST ME.
HELP ME WITH HER, MIKIL.
WHERE ARE WE GOING?
TO THE DESERT. WE RIDE TO THE DESERT.
I HAVE A LOT RIDING ON YOU, THOMAS OF HUNTER.

THE DESERT.
NOW WHERE?
THE NORTHERN CANYON LANDS.
WE COULD LOSE THEM FOR GOOD THERE.
WE COULD LOSE OURSELVES FOR GOOD THERE.
WILL THE HORDE FIND US HERE, JOHAN?
NOT TONIGHT. BUT TOMORROW, YES. THEY WILL.
WE MAKE CAMP THEN. NO FIRES. TELL THE OTHERS.
THOMAS...
GO.
I LOVE YOU. I'LL ALWAYS LOVE YOU.
WHAT'S THAT?
IT'S HIM! IT'S JUSTIN!
GOOD AFTERNOON. HOW DID YOU LIKE THE LAKE?
FORGIVE ME.
I HAVE. AND YOU FOLLOWED ME, DIDN'T YOU?
I'VE SHOWN YOU MY MIND AND MY WAY, NOW I WILL SHOW YOU MY HEART.
BUT, RACHELLE...
IS IN GOOD HANDS. LAUGHING LIKE SHE USED TO IN THE LAKE.
THE GREAT ROMANCE IS FOR YOU. IF ONLY ONE OF YOU HAD FOLLOWED, THE HEAVENS WOULD NOT HAVE HELD BACK MY CRIES OF JOY.
I HAVE WAITED SO LONG FOR THIS DAY. SO LONG TO TAKE MY BRIDE. TO RESCUE HER.
TO RESCUE YOU.

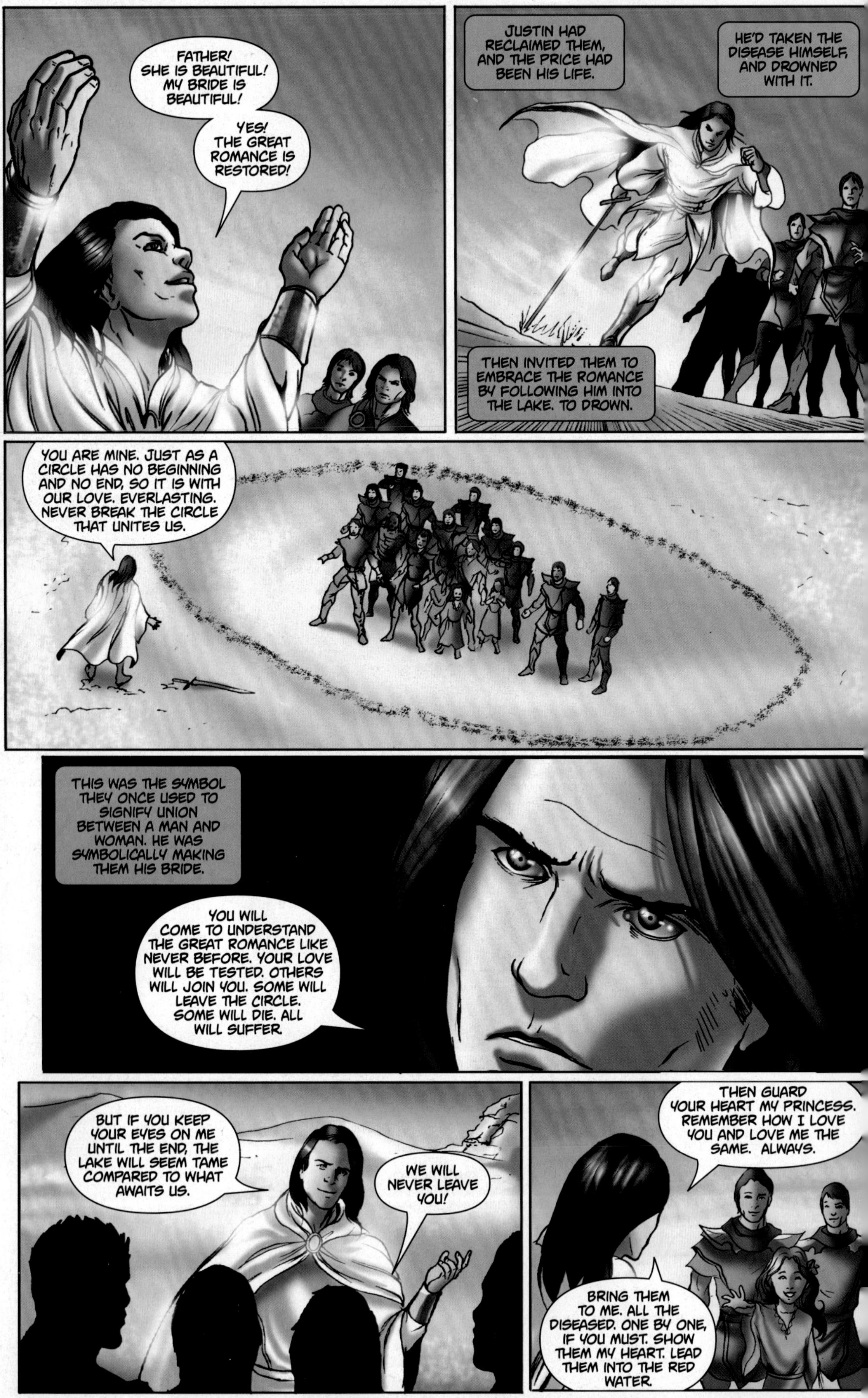
FATHER! SHE IS BEAUTIFUL! MY BRIDE IS BEAUTIFUL!
YES! THE GREAT ROMANCE IS RESTORED!
JUSTIN HAD RECLAIMED THEM, AND THE PRICE HAD BEEN HIS LIFE.
HE'D TAKEN THE DISEASE HIMSELF, AND DROWNED WITH IT.
THEN INVITED THEM TO EMBRACE THE ROMANCE BY FOLLOWING HIM INTO THE LAKE. TO DROWN.
YOU ARE MINE. JUST AS A CIRCLE HAS NO BEGINNING AND NO END, SO IT IS WITH OUR LOVE. EVERLASTING. NEVER BREAK THE CIRCLE THAT UNITES US.
THIS WAS THE SYMBOL THEY ONCE USED TO SIGNIFY UNION BETWEEN A MAN AND WOMAN. HE WAS SYMBOLICALLY MAKING THEM HIS BRIDE.
YOU WILL COME TO UNDERSTAND THE GREAT ROMANCE LIKE NEVER BEFORE. YOUR LOVE WILL BE TESTED. OTHERS WILL JOIN YOU. SOME WILL LEAVE THE CIRCLE. SOME WILL DIE. ALL WILL SUFFER.
BUT IF YOU KEEP YOUR EYES ON ME UNTIL THE END, THE LAKE WILL SEEM TAME COMPARED TO WHAT AWAITS US.
WE WILL NEVER LEAVE YOU!
THEN GUARD YOUR HEART MY PRINCESS. REMEMBER HOW I LOVE YOU AND LOVE ME THE SAME. ALWAYS.
BRING THEM TO ME. ALL THE DISEASED. ONE BY ONE, IF YOU MUST. SHOW THEM MY HEART. LEAD THEM INTO THE RED WATER.

DO YOU RECOGNIZE THIS BOOK, THOMAS?
A BOOK OF HISTORY.
The Story of History
THERE ARE THOUSANDS, NOT JUST THE FEW THAT QURONG CARRIES IN HIS TRUNKS. THIS IS ONLY ONE, BUT IT WILL GUIDE YOU.
READ IT WELL. LEARN FROM IT.
The Story of History
WHAT ABOUT THE BLANK BOOK THAT I HAVE? DOES IT HAVE A PURPOSE?
THE BLANK BOOKS. THERE ARE MANY OF THOSE AS WELL. THEY ARE VERY POWERFUL AND CREATE HISTORY, BUT ONLY *IN* THE HISTORIES. HERE THEY ARE POWERLESS. ONE DAY YOU WILL UNDERSTAND.
IN THE MEANTIME, GUARD THE ONE YOU HAVE— IN THE WRONG HANDS IT COULD WREAK HAVOC.
NOW I MUST GO. KEEP YOUR HEARTS STRONG AND TRUE. FOLLOW THE WAY OF THE BOOK I HAVE LEFT WITH YOU. NEVER LEAVE THE CIRCLE. NEVER BREAK IT, AND I WILL BE WITH YOU ALWAYS.
WAIT. IF THIS BOOK WORKS ONLY IN THE HISTORIES, THEN THE HISTORIES ARE REAL? THE VIRUS?
AM I A BOY, THOMAS? AM I A LAMB OR A LION?
YOU ARE FATHER AND A SON.
WILL I DREAM AGAIN?
DID YOU EAT THE FRUIT LAST NIGHT?
NO.
WELL THEN...
REMEMBER, NEVER LEAVE THE CIRCLE.

WASHINGTON, D.C.
THIS HAD BETTER BE IMPORTANT.
YES MR. PRESIDENT, IT IS.
IT'S THE ISRAELIS.
THEY'VE LAUNCHED A MISSILE INTO THE BAY OF BISCAY. A WARNING SHOT.
THE NEXT ONE GOES INTO THE NAVAL BASE AT BREST.
THEY'VE GIVEN FRANCE 24 HOURS TO GUARANTEE ISRAEL'S SURVIVAL.
ANY RESPONSE FROM PARIS?
THEY'VE... RETALIATED.
THERE'S A MISSILE HEADED OVER THE MEDITERRANEAN. WE DON'T KNOW IT'S TARGET EITHER, OR IF IT'S JUST ANOTHER WARNING SHOT. ETA, THIRTY MINUTES... THAT WAS FOUR MINUTES AGO.
THEN IT'S BEGUN. GOD HELP US ALL, RON.
GOD HELP US ALL.

THE BODY HAD RESTED IN THE SEALED ROOM FOR NEARLY THREE DAYS.
HE'S DEAD. AS DEAD AS ANY MAN CARLOS HAD EVER KILLED.
THIS TIME THERE WAS NO MISTAKE.
THOMAS HUNTER WAS DEAD.
THERE'S NOTHING YOU CAN DO TO STOP US NOW HUNTER.
TIME TO FINISH WHAT THEY HAD ALL STARTED.
TO BE CONTINUED

DIVE DEEPER INTO
THE CIRC
A NEW YOUNG ADULT SERIES
FOR FANS OF BLACK, RED & WHITE
DIVE DEEPER WITH TED DEKKER
Beware to those who open this book...
A CIRCLE NOVEL
CHOSEN
NEW YORK TIMES BEST-SELLING AU
TED DEKKE
The betrayer is among us...
A CIRCLE NOVEL
INFIDEL
NEW YORK TIMES BEST-SELLING AUTHOR
TED DEKKER
AVAILABLE WHERE BOOKS ARE SOLD